LIFE LESSONS

BOOK TWO

LIGHT TRAVEL: LESSONS FROM THE FIELD

"We don't love people because they are perfect--such a person does not exist. We love people because God made them. Every single person was fashioned in the image of God. For that reason alone, everyone is valuable and should be treated as such." *Pamela Walton*

Ye are the light of the world. A city that is set on a hill cannot be hid.
Matt 5:14

Say not ye, There are yet four months, and then cometh harvest? behold, I say unto you, Lift up your eyes, and look on the fields; for they are white already to harvest.
John 4:35

Dedicated to God and my family

and

in memory of

Kalamity Jane Jacobson-

a favorite four-legged friend

who showered me with love and affection

...

you

are

missed

TABLE OF CONTENTS

*INDICATES A NAME HAS BEEN CHANGED

IN THE BEGINNING: PART TWO

There I sat. I don't know why it was at that particular moment that the words tumbled over my tongue and spilled out of my mouth but they did.

"I want to go to work for you full time, and I want *you* to pay me."

Instantly, my mind began to grapple with my already spoken request. 'Why would he want to hire me?' I thought. 'He is world renowned. Books are written about him. Many famous people work for him. People talk openly and at length about him, study him.' I had no idea that his answer to me would be yes, but yes it was. My principle appeal to him, I thought, would be that I was willing and available.

Life had been really hard for well over a decade. I had experienced a great deal of loss, and yet it was those losses that were now enabling me to go to work for him. I had been a divorced mother of two children, a teen-aged son and a little girl. Then my daughter died in an automobile accident when she was seven. Eight months later, I married the man of my dreams. Whirling in a sea of emotions ranging from the depths of despair over the loss of my daughter and the epitome of joy at having married the love of my life, once again tragedy hit. My husband had also been fatally injured in an automobile accident. My son, now grown, was out of the house.

Through a series of tragic circumstances, I had become unencumbered. Years before, I had flown from the sanctity of my parents' home while I was yet a teen--straight into the arms of married life. Reality now whispered softly in my ear; it was the first time I had ever been free.

I wrestled with this foreign state of being--torn between despair at the tragedies suffered and perplexed at the opportunities those losses now permitted. Nothing was stopping me from going anywhere, at any time. As terrible as it sounds, I thought that what I was feeling must be somewhat similar to that which a prisoner might feel upon being released from a penitentiary.

I had been accountable to or responsible for someone my entire life. What now? Life was a new page ready to be written with a multitude of possibilities. That was what made the request tumble from my lips. I *could* go to work for him now.

Intrigued, you ask; "Who *is* this famous employer?" My request for employment had been presented to…Jesus. And other than my decision to return to my Christian faith several years before, it would become the best decision I have ever made.

I wonder why people often equate God and faith with mental images of life most boring. My experience working for Him has proven quite the opposite. It is electrifying to receive "assignments" from God and watch the miraculous happen. Working for Him has led to a very exciting life-- one filled with instances of witnessing resurrection life quickening those who were spiritually or emotionally dead.

Matthew 7:7: Ask, and it shall be given you; seek, and ye shall find; knock, and it shall be opened unto you:

LABORER OF LOVE

My first assigned task from the Lord was to travel from Tennessee to Fort Worth, Texas, where He led me to a Vietnam veteran who had lost himself in drunkenness for many years. All that changed when my "Employer" sent me with a message specifically for him.

He also led me to a young man filled with rage…and cruel intent.

He led me to a woman who was a victim of incest. He had a message for her.

He led me to those battling cancer, heart disease, alcohol, drugs, bondage of every kind…all to whom He was sending His message through a messenger who was simply willing to, "Go ye…" That is what we all are; we are His messengers, His ambassadors. How we represent Him becomes all important.

I had the unique ability of watching from the position of an insider; a position which all Christians can/may be privy if they are willing to accept His directive for them to, "Go." I watched with wonder as He performed big things, such as dramatic transformations and miraculous healings, and yet, small incidents were just as amazing.

For instance, once, as I approached a toll booth in New Jersey, that 'still small voice' spoke. "Pay for the person behind you." As I drove up and pulled out an extra dollar, the toll worker said, "The person in front of you just paid your toll." I had become an unwitting participant in a pre-arranged blessing game He had obviously orchestrated, fulfilling His daily motto for us; "Do unto others," this time by performing His original version of what modern day terminology refers to as "paying it forward."

Remember my request for God to pay me? I had been doing His work for several months before I returned home for a much-needed rest. Late one night the phone rang. The caller was a seamy, shady used car salesman I had known for several years. He always wore his shirt open, revealing a large Italian Horn necklace. A humorous guy, he once told me he had an old Vega station wagon he should give me. He said he could install flashing lights and loud speakers on the top that would announce, "FOLLOW ME TO THE REVIVAL!"

"Where have you been?" he asked, obviously upset by my unexplained absence. "I've been calling you for weeks!"

I told him I had been in the northeast; I asked why he had been calling.

"Ah, man! God's been on my case the whole time! He told me to give you a car and $400!"

"Hallelujah!" I shouted, laughing.

That was how I would be paid. I received cash, cars, clothing, furs, jewelry, food, hats, provision of all kinds and forms from many different people. I never told anyone my needs. My Employer knew what they were. (He supplies a lot of my wants too). I love seeing His taste. It's impeccable in every area.

That's one of the great benefits of working for Jesus. He sees everything, He knows everything and He is everywhere. People need help. People need Him. That's why He needs laborers of love. Asking Him to hire me has led to an amazing life.

Then saith he unto his disciples, The harvest truly is plenteous, but the labourers are few;

Pray ye therefore the Lord of the harvest, that he will send forth labourers into his harvest. (Matt 9:37-38).

THE GREAT COMMISSION

My first book, *Life Lessons Book One,* was a collection of Christian essays and articles I had written over the years coupled with a section which consisted of excerpts from my Memoir. This subsequent book tells some incredible stories and "God-incidences" encountered over several years of my life as I went "about my Father's business" on His harvest field.

This book also includes an essay commissioned by The Lord to be written through me on the subject of evangelism. I would list myself as co-author, but I pretty much just stopped doing whatever thing I was engrossed in at the moment and obeyed when He told me to, "STOP!" followed by,"WRITE!" Then He inspired the words/stories written…so I can't really take much credit other than the fact that He used my hand and my experiences. I have included the back-story and the essay itself at the end of this book.

THE CALL TO EVANGELISM

My decision to work for Jesus was not a new idea when I broached the subject that day in the comfort of my living room. I had been working for Him for many years at that point. In *Life Lessons: Book One,* I told of my trek on the road of the printed word, but I didn't address the other positions He led me to beforehand.

I have never been trained for any of the positions I was hired to fill. One that stands out in particular, was when I was hired to work in Public Relations, acquiring fleet accounts for an automotive service business. The Lord wanted me hired. I remember distinctly how it happened. I was resting comfortably on the couch at my mom's house when the Holy Spirit spoke.

"Buy the Sunday paper! Right now!"

"Why, Lord?"

"There's a job I want you to take."

I sent my son to the store to get the paper. The Sunday paper, the most popular issue, sold fast. He purchased the last copy, hence the urgency in the command to buy it, "Right now!" Opening the classified ad section, I scoured the ads and found no viable option.

"I don't see anything Lord."

"Look at the display ad."

I glanced down to one which seemed to stand out: Fleet Sales Manager Position Available.

'I don't even know what that is Lord! And it's an automotive mechanical shop! Are you kidding me?'

"Call them in the morning and make an appointment for an interview."

I interviewed with the two male owners. They were honest about someone who had interviewed before me. He was an extremely good candidate for the position they said, a married man with three children. He had been in that same field for many years.

Then there was me. I had no experience other than some sales positions in the past in completely different fields. The humorous part happened next. The owners couldn't help but laugh as they shared their selection process.

They were completely deadlocked with the decision, torn; one wanted the male and one wanted me. It was so difficult for them to make the decision that they were finally reduced to flipping a coin! They flipped it five times in a row. It landed in my favor every single time! I would never have thought of Jesus' divine will being played out in a coin toss, but oh well; it convinced them to hire me!

I soon found that the position would serve as a unique platform for the Lord to use me in evangelism. He continually sent me with a message or to pray for people at various businesses. In addition to getting accounts, I became spiritually intertwined in the lives of many people with whom I had contact. I will share two stories which stand out.

I had gone to a local power company to see the director about our company servicing their fleet of vehicles. The visit went well. I was pretty confident that he was going to use us. We shook hands; I left.

Several weeks later, I was at a Christian Business Persons luncheon. As I was listening intently to the speaker, the Holy Spirit told me to get up immediately and go see the director of the power company I had met weeks before.I thought it was going to look rather rude for me to leave right in the middle of the man's speech, but I chose to go ahead and obey the Lord.

I arrived at the power company. The secretary seemed perplexed by my entrance. I explained to her that I was not there on business; it was something personal. I needed to see the director.

"Well, an unscheduled visit is out of the ordinary. He has someone in his office currently but I will check."

She knocked lightly on his door and then entered his office. He told her he could see me in a few minutes. Not long afterward, I was ushered in. I began by explaining that I was not there in regard to business, or at least not "worldly" business.

I told him that the Lord had interrupted my luncheon and told me to go see him immediately. I explained that things like that were not uncommon in my experience, that when they happened there was usually an urgent reason. Oftentimes, it was that the person was going through a very difficult time and needed prayer. On the other hand, sometimes the Lord was simply trying to tell the individual that He had indeed heard their cry/prayer and that He was on the scene with His help, with His marvelous ability to rescue. After all, He is described as, "an ever-present help in trouble."

I said that most often, whoever the individual was that I was being sent to had cried out to God, generally around three to four weeks before I arrived. The look on his face was very telling, first shock and then amazement. Everything I had said to him had been occurring in his life. He had been extremely close to his father who had died unexpectedly only a few weeks before. He was exceedingly grief stricken over it but then he revealed that he had recently married. His wife had walked out on him right after the funeral. She wanted a divorce. His eyes welled with tears despite his attempts to keep them at bay.

His struggle, his emotional pain had become overwhelming. Having come in with the message that Jesus Christ was actively involved in his situation and that He sent me to tell him of His great love for him had a tremendous impact on both of us that day. I thanked God for his love for this wounded man. I thanked God for sending me.

During that same time period, I had been led to stop in at a hair salon. I explained to the owner that I represented an automobile service company; we would appreciate her business. The beautician laughed. She was the only person who worked there; she didn't have a fleet of vehicles to service. I smiled as I handed her my card.

"Well, you are still welcome to stop in when you need maintenance on your vehicle."

The next day, I went to a new café which had opened recently. The beautician walked in. I went over and greeted her. We both commented how serendipitous it seemed that we had never met until the previous day, and now we had run into each other again.

Not many days later, that 'still small voice' spoke.

"Go see her. Sing her the song, 'In The Middle of It All'."

I owned a fairly lightweight karaoke machine and microphone which I always kept in my car. I had sung in jails, churches and various types of gatherings for many years. I had even sung to drunks who showed up on my front porch periodically. Then I would pray for them.

My thoughts traveled back to the day I had purchased the soundtrack. I had gone to a local Christian bookstore and scanned the selections available, praying for the Lord to show me which song He wanted me to sing. My eyes kept landing on one soundtrack in particular. I argued with Him about it.

"I've never heard of that song."

"Buy it."

"But it's probably not in my key."

"Look."

I took it out. It was in my key, which was an unusual key. I put it back and kept looking. Finally, it fell at my feet.

"Okay, Okay, Lord. I'll buy it!"

The song was unusual. The lyrics were written from the Lord's perspective, as though He was singing the song to us, His children.

I walked into the salon. The beautician showed obvious surprise. She raised her eyebrows, silently questioning my presence.

"I know this is going to sound strange, but The Lord told me to come to your shop and sing you a song."

"Well, if *He* told you to do it--you'd better do it. Just let me put a few things away in the back room first."

"Ok. I'll go get my karaoke machine."

She sat down. I explained the background of the song, that it was unique. The lyrics were the Lord's words to us.

By the time I got to the chorus, she was already in tears. The lyrics spoke of His omnipresence, compassion and care:

"But in the middle of it all, I'm always close beside you-- to constantly remind you-- that it's from my strength you draw... and when the nights just linger on-- I'm not that far at all... I'll never let you fall... I hear you when you call... in the middle of it all."

We talked afterward. She said she had been raised a Christian all her life but she was in a backslidden state. She had married an ungodly, worldly man; they were getting a divorce. I told her that the Lord wanted her to know that He loved her, that He sent me specifically to sing the words in that song to her. I asked if she minded if I prayed for her.

"No. Go ahead. Please do. I need it."

We became fast friends and stayed that way for many years afterward. Her life was totally transformed. Her husband, who had been committing adultery, divorced her. Later, she met a godly Christian man whom she married. They have been married for many years and work together in the ministry.

COME AS A LITTLE CHILD (PART 2)

One of the things I shared in my first book was that my earthly father taught me the lesson: "always go straight to the top" with any questions/concerns I had. God is at the very top so I have formed the habit of going straight to Him about everything, from the little things, like a lost earring or a new dress for a special occasion, to big things; where do I go from here? How do I pray for this person and their burdens? Will I ever recover from this tragedy?

The wonderful thing about Jesus is that He is the *Father Extraordinaire*…You can't get any better than a Father who is with you always, has your best interests at heart, one with whom any correction meted out is never out of anger but borne out of a pure heart encapsulated in total goodness and with the ultimate desire and outcome being for you to have a better life. He is the only One who has the answer for everything you will ever encounter in life. Understanding this truth is one of the greatest lessons I have learned in my walk in life. When He said, "Come to me as a little child," I did.

It didn't happen overnight. I learned as I pondered His request. What was His point? I thought about the nature of children. They are *totally* dependent. The "world" calls us to, "be independent." A mentality steeped in the belief that the highest achievement sought after is to "be your own boss." One which promotes the philosophy, "Don't count on anyone but you," and, "look out for number one,"

21

meaning you--rather than God. It is a mindset in direct opposition to the mindset Christians are called to, and yet, many are still enmeshed in that skewed belief system.

I can't count the number of times I asked someone if they had prayed about a decision or situation, or even a small matter, something they couldn't find, and they responded, "Oh, I wouldn't bother God with something like that!" What do they think they're going to do--overwhelm God? I can hear Jesus now. "Listen, I'm really sorry, but I just can't handle one more thing right now. I have far too much on My plate. You handle it."

Lest I come across as being judgmental, speaking on their behalf, I do believe that this mode of thinking is often looked upon as reverence-based and prudent at its core, (although it is an unfortunate misapprehension), Their requests weighed in light of their own finite understanding, their prayers reserved for those deemed more urgent, larger matters. However, it's a pretty silly notion when viewed from the Lord's perspective.

Why would you want to make a series of wrong decisions and then finally, when you have messed things up so badly that you find yourself in dire straits-- then, and only then, you decide to seek the Lord? Why would you search for hours or days for something lost, wasting valuable time when He knows right where it is? It's not bright. Go to Him first about everything and you will have far fewer messes…

After discussing the subject with some fellow members of a writers group, one friend summed up the problem by posing a humorous rhetorical question; "Yes, why ask for God's help when you have only one foot steeped in dung. Wait until you have both in it!"

Let me give a couple further examples of two Biblical exhortations which are intricately intertwined: "come as a little child," and, "ask and ye shall receive."

Why bother God in *ALL* our ways? This happened. My mother needed an item in her house replaced. She was a widow. (Jesus really looks out for widows. The book of James lists looking out for widows and orphans as evidence of pure religion). I had been taught by God to pray about everything, so I prayed about my mother's need. Not only did she get the best price available on the item, but while there, we ran into someone who, unbeknownst to me, was having a terrible time struggling with depression. I was able to give her some "words fitly spoken" as the Bible refers to them, and offered to pray for her.

Weeks later, we ran into each other again. She told me how touched she was by our conversation and the resulting prayer. I didn't know it at the time, but she had been experiencing suicidal thoughts. It was a divine appointment. Rather than calling every store in town and driving all over the city, we were led to the best deal in town and then Jesus was able to come to the rescue of one of His children by sending a member of His body to minister to her.

One Saturday years ago, the pump which pumped spring water to my house quit working. Parts and labor would not be available until Monday. I went directly to Jesus about my situation.

"Lord, I am your bride. No husband wants his bride to go without water for an entire week end!" I whined.

"It's the same principle as a corroded battery in your car," His wonderful 'still small voice' responded. "Contact is not being made. Take a brush and baking soda and clean the contacts."

I quickly grabbed the items, made haste down to the pump house, followed His directions, flipped the switch and VOILA'; I had water! I have shared that story many times throughout the years, using it to teach others of the often untapped "Source" we have in Jesus, who delights in helping His children.

I was sharing this lesson with a friend of mine years ago. Ann* seemed to continually poor-mouth, as it is referred to in the south.

"Pam, I'm just a poor woman. I ain't got much."

She constantly had needs which were seemingly unmet. I began responding to her statements with what the Word of God says.

"Stop saying that!" I exhorted. "Our father owns the cattle on a thousand hills! King David said, 'I once was young and now I'm old, but I have never seen the righteous forsaken, nor his seed begging bread.' If you have a need, go to God with it! Ask Him! Quit poor mouthing and asking people for things."

Ann learned to ask the Lord, although it took a while. A couple incidences come to mind.

Ann stopped by to see me one day. She told me she needed glasses but couldn't afford them.

"Did you ask the Lord?"

"About that?"

"Yes. Remember? About everything!"

We prayed.

The next time I saw her, she showed me a pair of 14K gold antique glasses she had received in exchange for painting a sign. (She told me she didn't even know how to paint. She said the Lord had provided the job). They were the perfect prescription for her eyes. The word "LORD" was written on the inside.

"Wow. That's amazing!"

"There's only one problem, Pam. The piece that curls around the ear is missing."

"Ask the Lord."

She prayed.

A few days later, Ann was sitting in a truck with her ex-husband. She explained that I had been teaching her to pray about everything. She showed him the glasses the Lord had provided as proof that the concept was working. The only thing lacking, she told him, was the curled ear piece. He eyed her with skepticism.

Just then, something flew in through the passenger window and landed on her. Ann picked up a curved piece of metal; startled and curious, she unfolded it. It was the piece she needed for her glasses.

Another time I was driving back to Tennessee from Alabama. The Lord spoke to me.

"Call Ann.* Give her some money." I called her.

"How much money do you need?" I asked.

"Pam? Where are you? Are you outside the bathroom of my trailer?"

"No, I'm driving back from Alabama. I'm about an hour and a half away. Why?"

"Because, Pam, you told me that we are supposed to go into our prayer closet and pray to the Lord. This trailer is so small, there's no closet I can pray in. So I went into the bathroom to pray. I said, 'Lord, Pam told me that I'm supposed to ask you for everything. I need some money so I'm asking you for it'. I just said that and now you call and ask how much money I need! I thought you must be outside my bathroom and heard me ask the Lord for money."

"Nope," I laughed. "I was driving along when suddenly, the Lord said to call you. He wants me to give you some money. I just didn't know how much."

That's how He works. He blesses in the natural and the supernatural all at once. He is all-knowing. Why rely on your petty, finite, carnal mind rather than that of The Omniscient One? No matter how bright you think your light bulb is, figure it out--you don't know more than God Almighty. If you think you do, there's your proof right there.

Matt 18:2-4 And Jesus called a little child unto him, and set him in the midst of them, And said, Verily I say unto you, Except ye be converted, and become as little children, ye shall not enter into the kingdom of heaven.Whosoever therefore shall humble himself as this little child, the same is greatest in the kingdom of heaven.

DREAMS AND VISIONS

And the LORD visited Hannah, so that she conceived, and bare three sons and two daughters. And the child Samuel grew before the LORD.

And the child Samuel grew on, and was in favour both with the LORD, and also with men.

And the child Samuel ministered unto the LORD before Eli. And the word of the LORD was precious in those days; there was no open vision.

And ere the lamp of God went out in the temple of the LORD, where the ark of God was, and Samuel was laid down to sleep;

That the LORD called Samuel: and he answered, Here am I.

And the LORD called yet again, Samuel. And Samuel arose and went to Eli, and said, Here am I; for thou didst call me. And he answered, I called not, my son; lie down again.

Now Samuel did not yet know the LORD, neither was the word of the LORD yet revealed unto him.

And the LORD called Samuel again the third time. And he arose and went to Eli, and said, Here am I; for thou didst call me. And Eli perceived that the LORD had called the child.

Therefore Eli said unto Samuel, Go, lie down: and it shall be, if he call thee, that thou shalt say, Speak, LORD;

for thy servant heareth. So Samuel went and lay down in his place.

And the LORD came, and stood, and called as at other times, Samuel, Samuel. Then Samuel answered, Speak; for thy servant heareth.

And the LORD said to Samuel, Behold, I will do a thing in Israel, at which both the ears of every one that heareth it shall tingle.

And Samuel lay until the morning, and opened the doors of the house of the LORD. And Samuel feared to shew Eli the vision.

Then Eli called Samuel, and said, Samuel, my son. And he answered, Here am I.

And Samuel told him every whit, and hid nothing from him. And he said, It is the LORD: let him do what seemeth him good.

And Samuel grew, and the LORD was with him, and did let none of his words fall to the ground.

And all Israel from Dan even to Beersheba knew that Samuel was established to be a prophet of the LORD. (1Samuel 2:21,26, 3:1,3,4,6-10,11,15,16,18-20)

I had a very close, intimate relationship with God from the time I was very young. I would go for walks in the woods and tell Him how awesome He was. To this day, I reserve the term *awesome* only in reference to God or His wonderful creation. You won't hear me say how "awesome" getting a good deal on some material object is.

By definition, the word "awesome" is something awe-inspiring. Most of the instances in which it is currently used fall rather short of being awe-inspiring.

Every enormous tree with its thick, powerful overhanging limbs and rough bark, every bug and crawling creature inspired my awe. How did He think of these things? Pondering a mind which could create every single system in every living thing was mind-boggling to me.

I also had such a relationship with Him that I couldn't wait for my parents to leave the room at night after we said our simple little prayers together. It was then that I *communed* with my Heavenly Father upon my bed. It's nothing new-Samuel the prophet (as noted above) was called by God when he was a mere child.

I don't know if it was the type of relationship that we had which propelled me into having prophetic dreams and visions, but it began when I was very young and has never stopped. This is not psychic stuff. They are revelation gifts listed in Acts chapter 2:17-18 and I Corinthians, chapter 12, in the New Testament.

Act 2:17 And it shall come to pass in the last days, saith God, I will pour out of my Spirit upon all flesh: and your sons and your daughters shall prophesy, and your young men shall see visions, and your old men shall dream dreams:
Act 2:18 And on my servants and on my handmaidens I will pour out in those days of my Spirit; and they shall prophesy:

1Co 12:1 Now concerning spiritual gifts, brethren, I would not have you ignorant.

1Co 12:7 But the manifestation of the Spirit is given to every man to profit withal.

1Co 12:8 For to one is given by the Spirit the word of wisdom; to another the word of knowledge by the same Spirit;

1Co 12:9 To another faith by the same Spirit; to another the gifts of healing by the same Spirit;

1Co 12:10 To another the working of miracles; to another prophecy; to another discerning of spirits; to another divers kinds of tongues; to another the interpretation of tongues:

1Co 12:11 But all these worketh that one and the selfsame Spirit, dividing to every man severally as he will.

One distinct vision I had which is indelibly imprinted in my mind to this day, occurred when I was nine years old. I saw a vision of the most beautiful, plush tree I had ever seen. It was virtually indescribable. I have never seen anything like it. It had twelve different types of fruit hanging on it. Amazed by the sight, I questioned the Lord.

"What is that?"

"It is the Tree of Life, which is in the midst of the Paradise of God."

Satisfied, but without understanding, I then asked about the fruit hanging on it. He said they represented the twelve tribes of Israel. I had never heard of either the Paradise of God or the Twelve Tribes of Israel; I was only nine years old, but I loved seeing the vision and especially the fact that He had shown it to me.

I continue to have prophetic dreams and visions almost nightly, and consider them precious gifts. As stated in the Word of God, Jesus shows us things in dreams and visions. These gifts are available to all believers.

I was with a friend once when the topic of spiritual dreams came up. She said she used to have prophetic dreams years before, when she was a child but they had left her long ago. I still remember vividly what transpired afterward, as we stood on her front porch on a Friday evening.

"Well, why don't we pray for the dreams to start back up? It says in His word that He wants to show us things to come."

"OK."

We prayed right then. The dreams came in abundance-- prophetic dreams of every kind. There were dreams of things that would take place at our church in the future, warning dreams, and marvelously unfolding revelations of the Lord's involvement in people's lives.

If you too, want to have dreams and visions--just ask. He is listening, watching, waiting for you to ask Him to be an integral, active partner with you in what He refers to as,"abundant life." All that is required is for you to ask.

(Matthew 7:7: Ask, and it shall be given you ;)

When the Lord accepted my application to work for Him full-time, the prophetic dreams took an unusual turn. I began dreaming about every trip He was preparing me to go on; I saw the people I would meet, the events I would attend and the places I would visit—all beforehand.

And it shall come to pass in the last days, saith God, I will pour out of my Spirit upon all flesh: and your sons and your daughters shall prophesy, and your young men shall see visions, and your old men shall dream dreams: (Acts 2:17)

THE BODY OF CHRIST

I have often attended a gathering held in Bethany, Connecticut. People come from all over to play, listen to, or sing in a barn owned by a Columbia University educated retired physician who sports gray dreadlocks and calls Contra dancing. His barn-turned-into-home is filled with talented musicians of every genre-- one evening per month. The last time I attended, I stood where those who are long-time residents of Tennessee (or in rural parts of the South in general) all know is the best location in a home when the weather is chilly. I was backed up to a wood burning heater, one which had a simmering pot of apple cider resting on its top. A young man dressed in an outfit fashioned out of deerskin struck up a conversation.

"Have you been here before?"

"Yes, many times. It's great!"

"It definitely is!"

"That's an interesting outfit you have on."

"I made it. It is made from a road kill deer, which I tanned and sewed myself."

"Wow. That's great. What do you do?"

"I run a wilderness healing recovery program. What do you do?"

"I'm an evangelist sent from Tennessee to Connecticut."

"Interesting; do you preach in churches here?"

"Sometimes I speak, but mainly I go out and about to the highways and byways, to people God sends me to."

"Really? You go to people one by one then?"

"Yes, to those I am sent."

"Ah! You are a white blood cell!"

"A white blood cell?"

"Yes. When there is infection or disease in the body, the white blood cell races to the scene, bringing healing. You are a white blood cell."

"Wow. That is one of the coolest compliments anyone has ever given me! Thank you. Do you mind if I use this conversation and what you just said? I'm writing a book. I want to put this in it!"

The conversation served as a catalyst, a jump start to my mind racing in the direction of the Lord's likening us to a body, His Body, made up of differing parts which are all needed, all necessary for the proper functioning of the whole. I posted the story on facebook. A friend commented that as an evangelist, I was actually, "A red blood cell-- bringing oxygen to sustain life."

I began pondering the Body of Christ and its parts. Although the parts all differ, they all have something in common--all carry red and white blood cells within them. So, all of us are carrying what it takes to bring healing and sustain life. The following testimonies chronicle the lives of some of those to whom I was sent--serving as either a white blood cell, bringing His miraculous healing or as a red blood cell, bringing the breath/inspiration of God to those who needed life.

For as the body is one, and hath many members, and all the members of that one body, being many, are one body: so also is Christ.

For by one Spirit are we all baptized into one body, whether we be Jews or Gentiles, whether we be bond or free; and have been all made to drink into one Spirit.

For the body is not one member, but many.

If the foot shall say, Because I am not the hand, I am not of the body; is it therefore not of the body?

And if the ear shall say, Because I am not the eye, I am not of the body; is it therefore not of the body?

If the whole body were an eye, where were the hearing? If the whole were hearing, where were the smelling?

But now hath God set the members every one of them in the body, as it hath pleased him.

And if they were all one member, where were the body?

But now are they many members, yet but one body.

And the eye cannot say unto the hand, I have no need of thee: nor again the head to the feet, I have no need of you.

Nay, much more those members of the body, which seem to be more feeble, are necessary:

And those members of the body, which we think to be less honourable, upon these we bestow more abundant honour; and our uncomely parts have more abundant comeliness.

For our comely parts have no need: but God hath tempered the body together, having given more abundant honour to that part which lacked:

That there should be no schism in the body; but that the members should have the same care one for another.

And whether one member suffer, all the members suffer with it; or one member be honoured, all the members rejoice with it.

Now ye are the body of Christ, and members in particular.

And God hath set some in the church, first apostles, secondarily prophets, thirdly teachers, after that miracles, then gifts of healings, helps, governments, diversities of tongues.

Are all apostles? are all prophets? are all teachers? are all workers of miracles?

Have all the gifts of healing? do all speak with tongues? do all interpret?

But covet earnestly the best gifts: and yet shew I unto you a more excellent way.(I Cor 12:12-31).

TURNIP GREEN TESTIMONY

The phone rang. It was my friend Lynn.* She had been living in Fort Worth for about seven or eight years. I had not heard from her in a long time. I was taken aback by her call. I remember it was in early March.

"Wow!" my surprise burst forth. "I haven't heard from you in ages!"

"Well," she began, "Randy* (her husband) needs help and you were the first person who came to mind. He has a car lot with about 13 to15 cars on it that he needs to liquidate so he can sell the business right away. I remembered that you could sell anything so I thought I would invite you down for a few weeks. You could stay with us. We could catch up and talk about old times, and since you could sell ice cream to Eskimos, I figured you could use your persuasive talents to get rid of the cars he hasn't been able to sell."

I appreciated her confidence in my sales ability and thought how nice it would be to see her again but unfortunately, I didn't "bear witness" that it was something I should do. I told her I would pray about it. Some Christians say that they will "pray about" a matter when it's something they don't want to do. That wasn't the case. I felt neutral about her request but I really didn't think I was going to get the go ahead from God. I prayed. As suspected, His answer was "No."

Fast forward. It was months later. During this time period, the Lord had been repeatedly bringing a scripture to my mind. I began meditating on it. It was Psalm 37:4, "Delight thyself also in the Lord; and he shall give thee the desires of thine heart." I kept thinking about it.

"How do I do such a thing?" I inquired of the Lord. "What do you mean when you say, 'delight thyself in the Lord'? I mean, does delighting myself in you constitute my praising you? Singing to you? You tell me to do this in your Word but you don't tell me *how*."

He answered immediately.

"Read Isaiah chapter 58."

With a mixture of curiosity and fascination, I turned to the chapter. I glanced at the heading; "The Fast of the Lord." I hadn't bothered to read the text yet, but having read the chapter heading alone, my reaction was astonishment.

"You mean *fasting* is the way to delight myself in you? I need to *fast*? You want me to go without food in order to delight myself in you?"

"Read the chapter," He said.

Wow. Talk about some revelation knowledge. For years, I had heard numerous teachings on fasting. This chapter dispelled all that I had been taught. The fast of the Lord had a totally different definition in that chapter. He begins with a treatise against the transgressions and sins of

His people. He then does a commentary on their fasting. "Is this the fast that I have chosen?" He asks, before describing their actions, their mistaken idea of what true fasting looks like. Then He describes *HIS* definition of fasting in verses 6-14.

Is not this the fast that I have chosen? to loose the bands of wickedness, to undo the heavy burdens, and to let the oppressed go free, and that ye break every yoke?

Is it not to deal thy bread to the hungry, and that thou bring the poor that are cast out to thy house? when thou seest the naked, that thou cover him; and that thou hide not thyself from thine own flesh?

Then shall thy light break forth as the morning, and thine health shall spring forth speedily: and thy righteousness shall go before thee; the glory of the LORD shall be thy rereward.

Then shalt thou call, and the LORD shall answer; thou shalt cry, and he shall say, Here I am. If thou take away from the midst of thee the yoke, the putting forth of the finger, and speaking vanity;

And if thou draw out thy soul to the hungry, and satisfy the afflicted soul; then shall thy light rise in obscurity, and thy darkness be as the noonday:

And the LORD shall guide thee continually, and satisfy thy soul in drought, and make fat thy bones: and thou shalt be like a watered garden, and like a spring of water, whose waters fail not.

And they that shall be of thee shall build the old waste places: thou shalt raise up the foundations of many generations; and thou shalt be called, The repairer of the breach, The restorer of paths to dwell in.

If thou turn away thy foot from the sabbath, from doing thy pleasure on my holy day; and call the sabbath a delight, the holy of the LORD, honourable; and shalt honour him, not doing thine own ways, nor finding thine own pleasure, nor speaking thine own words:

Then shalt thou delight thyself in the LORD; and I will cause thee to ride upon the high places of the earth, and feed thee with the heritage of Jacob thy father: for the mouth of the LORD hath spoken it. (Isa 58:6-14).

I was astounded (although I should not have been) when my eyes landed on verse 14a; the beginning of the first sentence of the last scripture in the chapter. *Isa 58:14 "Then shalt thou delight thyself in the LORD;"*

What was more shocking to me than the revelation the Lord had shown me about His definition of fasting was my verbal reaction.

"But I've been doing that, Lord."

I couldn't believe I said that to Him but it was true. I had, over a span of several years, and through His strength, done a lot of those things. Our conversation ended.

Months later, I was in my living room. I had told the Lord I wanted to go to work for Him full-time, and I wanted Him to pay me. I remember how He told me His answer. A couple of days later, I was sitting on the couch watching Joyce Meyer on television. As always, at the end of the program the announcer broadcast where she would be holding upcoming conferences. When he announced that she would be in Ft. Worth, Texas, the Lord spoke.

"Go to the conference."

I thought, 'Really? When?' He said He would let me know when to leave. After His directive, I began hearing sermon after sermon--all based on one scripture. "Not by might, nor by power, but by my spirit, saith the LORD of hosts." (Zechariah 4:6).

My first thought was Lynn. She had asked me to come and help her several months prior, and His answer had been no. Now, I wanted to call and ask if she would put me up. She answered the phone.

"Hey, it's me." I tried to sound chipper.

"Hi. What's up?" Her response lacked oomph.

"Well, I'm going to be coming to Fort Worth soon, and wondered if I could stay at your place while I'm there."

"Why now? I asked you to come before and you said the Lord said no."

"I don't know why now and not then, Lynn. I was sitting in my living room and the Lord told me to go to the Joyce Meyer conference in Fort Worth. Ever heard of her?"

"No, but it's not a good time."

I wondered if Lynn was mad at me over my not coming before when she needed me.

"I won't be a bother; I will stay out of your way. It starts on a Thursday evening and goes through Saturday. I could visit your mom in Oklahoma for a day or two prior, then come to your place on Wednesday and leave on Sunday."

"It's not a good time."

"You don't want to see me?"

I was surprised by her response. Her rejection and lack of desire to have me come visit was starting to hurt. I thought she would love to see me. We had been very close for many years.

"It's not that. Well...It's Randy. We're getting a divorce."

"No way!"

"Yes, I haven't told you this, but he's an alcoholic and I can't take it anymore. It's been going on the entire time we have been married, ten years. I just can't do it anymore. I would love to see you, but it's very uncomfortable. He's moving out that very week end."

"Please let me come! God told me to. There is always a reason why. I really feel like I'm supposed to..."

"Well, like I said, I would love to see you, but I can't guarantee it will be much fun. Things are very tense right now."

"I don't care. I just want to see you--despite the situation, and because the Lord told me to come. I will see you that Wednesday before the conference."

"OK. Have a safe trip. Be careful. I love you."

I was relieved. I would be able to obey the Lord; whatever it was that He wanted to accomplish through me would be accomplished. I had persevered, almost forcing myself as Lynn's houseguest. I turned on the television. A preacher cried out, "It's not by might, nor by power, but by my Spirit saith the Lord!" I thought, "Wow. It seems like everyone is quoting that scripture lately.' It had been one of my favorite scriptures through the years.

Permission received, all I had to do now was ask the Lord when I should leave. I packed up my car and got ready to leave. I would stay one night on the road and two nights in Oklahoma at my friend's family farm before making the trek down to Dallas.

The Lord told me to leave on a Sunday. I would be travelling through Nashville and felt impressed that I should visit my former pastor's church there. It was an all-black church with the exception of me that day.

There have been certain little material desires of my heart that bring a smile to my face when I receive them or when I think of them. I think back to my childhood experience. I became accustomed to receiving small gifts, little presents because my dad would bring me a surprise every time he'd come back from a trip somewhere. Dad would arrive and inevitably, he would pull out some special thing that I liked, animal crackers or something he had picked up just to let me know that he been thinking of me.

I can never get enough perfume. I love perfume, which is why I run out of it very fast. One of my favorites at the time was *Passion* by Elizabeth Taylor, although I usually bought the dollar store knock off. Any time I wore it, I received lots of compliments. It went well with my chemistry. I also have particular food cravings.I like the little fish-shaped crackers called Whales. I sometimes crave turnip greens.

I like clothing of all types. One particular style I like is a knee-length black velvet off-the-shoulder fitted dress for evening wear. I had been thinking about one I had seen years before that my boss's wife wore to a Christmas party. It was beautiful.

I traveled to Nashville, arrived at the church and sat down. The people were wonderful, the praise and worship was vibrant and the sermon was inspirational. There was only one problem. The entire time I was sitting there, my mind kept drifting to turnip greens. It was all I could think about. I was craving them! At the end of the service an announcement was made for all the singles to stay for a brief meeting.

The Pastor approached me and told me how nice it was to have me visiting that day. He asked if I had enjoyed the service. I confessed my wandering mind and its important focus--turnip greens. He was very gracious and offered to take me to a local restaurant along with his beautiful wife whereupon I could have my desire fulfilled.

"No thank you. I want them homemade somewhere, somehow. It's just different. But I really appreciate your generous offer."

He smiled understandingly, asked if I was sure, noted my nod of assent and left. The exchange left me lingering in the sanctuary long enough to catch the singles meeting. I caught snippets of the overview from the woman in charge. There was a lunch being held for all the singles in a few minutes at "Rosetta's house." She was cooking a huge pot of homemade turnip greens along with a vast array of great food. The young woman said, "All the singles are invited." There was one problem. They needed one more car to transport some of the singles to the luncheon.

'Turnip Greens!!!' I thought.

"I'm single and I have a car! Can I come?" I yelled across at the group gathered.

She looked at me, cocked her head to the side, placed her hands on her hips and smiled broadly.

"I said, '*ALL*' singles are invited!" She emphasized.

46

Praise God! I was getting homemade greens! It was a quick ride there. I couldn't get over the amount of wonderful food. A huge pot of greens was simmering on the stove, along with an equally large pot of black-eyed peas. Perfectly baked corn bread, the sweet kind that I prefer awaited my now salivating palate, as well as an abundance of crispy fried chicken. Large containers of homemade lemonade graced the tables. I felt like I had died and gone to Southern Cookin' Heaven.

Rides had been arranged afterward; my car was no longer needed. The members were very nice and sent me on my way with prayer. I was amazed by Jesus' care for my seemingly unimportant desire and the degree to which I had experienced His provision.

I got on the road and headed toward Oklahoma. I turned on the radio as Joyce Meyer's program was ending. "Remember, it's not by might, nor by power, but by my Spirit says the Lord." She asserted boldly. I thought, 'How many times am I going to hear this?'

I stopped at a convenience store to get a cup of coffee. After pouring a large, piping hot cup, I walked to the counter to pay for my drink.

"How much do I owe you?" I asked the female clerk.

"Nothing."

"Really? Nothing? But I have a large coffee here."

"You don't owe anything. It's on me." A male co-worker stood beside her, smiling.

I was dumbfounded. I had never received anything from a convenience store for free. I thanked them profusely and drove back onto the highway. Several hours down the road, I stopped for the night and rented a room at a motel.

The next morning, I started the last leg of my trip. Having stopped for gas, I glanced in the mirror. I Freshened my face and made a mental note that I was low on my favorite lipstick. Passing a multitude of farms and rich countryside, I noticed as cattle glanced my way occasionally. The ride was rather uneventful. As the miles ticked off, I conversed with the only one in the car with me. "Lord, I didn't realize that I'm almost out of my favorite lipstick."

I arrived at the family farm in the early afternoon. I was greeted warmly by Lynn's mother. It had been seven years since I had seen her, but as it is with some long term friends, it felt as though no time had elapsed. I sat down at the kitchen table. I started to speak but was quickly interrupted when I saw a "light bulb just went off" look flash across her face

"Do you need lipstick?"

Before I could answer, she looked at me and gave a slight nod.

"Wait here a minute."

She scurried down the hallway, arriving back within a minute. She held up two tubes of lipstick in the exact shade as the one I told the Lord I was running out of. I couldn't believe it. Other than the "hello after all these years" greeting a few minutes before, I hadn't exchanged a word with her and it wasn't as though my lips were bare; I had lipstick on.

Since I had spent many vacations in their home town through the years, Lynn and her brother's friends had become my friends as well. Her brother took me around. We visited them and caught up on what had been happening in their lives. I had known most of the people before becoming a Christian. I had not seen many of them since.

One of the mutual friends had married. He and his wife had adopted a foster child. Later, they adopted the child's sibling. He asked for prayer because there were two more siblings they were hoping to adopt. I agreed to pray. Soon afterward, I learned that the request had been granted. It seemed as though I was receiving a multitude of prayer requests from unlikely people and not only was that unusual, but it was also very heartening as I heard reports of the prayers being answered quickly, miraculously.

I left Oklahoma on Wednesday as promised and headed to Ft. Worth. Again, I turned on the radio and heard several ministers preach on that same scripture again, what I refer to now as the "theme scripture" for the trip. (Every "God trip" I have been sent on since being hired by Him has had a theme scripture).

The one given for this trip, "Not by might, nor by power, but by my Spirit, saith the LORD of hosts," was a good one. God was up to something, something good, and something that could only be accomplished by His Spirit. I began to get excited, and although prayers had already been offered up and answered, I felt like the scripture was referring to something which had not yet taken place.

I was greeted with a warm hug. Lynn and I walked into her den. She opened up about the ten years of hell she had been experiencing living with an alcoholic. She said they needed to sell their house but it wasn't ready. Years of working long hours and her struggle with situational depression had taken a toll on her surroundings.

Thursday morning she left for work. I had been decorating and performing design remix/ visual coordinating since I was in grade school, so my brain began to take in its surroundings. I saw what changes needed to be made to stage the home. Diving into the work, I was interrupted by a call from Lynn, who had taken a moment to check on me during her lunch hour. I confessed my activity in her absence, qualifying it with a promise that if she didn't like the changes made by my staging efforts, I would change everything back, although I was quite confident that she would love what she saw.

Lynn returned to a transformed room. She loved the work I had performed and thinking aloud, whispered, "I wish the whole house could be done." Those were the words I was waiting to hear! I was like a staging mad woman--tackling the entire house while she was at work over the next few days. The place looked amazing, so much so, she offered to buy me some expensive cologne and pay me for my work. I told her I didn't feel like she was supposed to buy me perfume, even though I like receiving it and it didn't make sense for me to turn down the offer of a free gift.

She shook her head, and then said, "Wait here." She returned with a huge stack of beautiful clothes. Evening wear included a vintage Morty Sussman gown designed for the Mollie Parnis Boutique (Their gowns have been worn by several First ladies) and an off-the shoulder, black velvet knee-length dress. The stack was several feet high and they were all my size.

"Take these. I want you to have them. I will never wear them."

I was flabbergasted. Every clothing desire I had ever had was right there in front of me! And free of charge! God was very good to me.

Thursday evening, I went to the large church for the beginning of Joyce Meyer's three day conference. It was a good service. I was ripe with anticipation for what I knew would be another great teaching. A woman sat down beside me and began making small talk.

"Hi. Are you from around here?"

"No. I live in Tennessee, about an hour from Nashville."

"Really? Doesn't Joyce Meyer hold conferences in Nashville?"

"Yes, she does but I have never attended them."

"That doesn't make sense. I would think you would have just waited and gone locally rather than come all the way to Ft. Worth Texas!"

"Well God sent me here. He told me He wanted me to come to this one. In fact, prior to leaving and all the way here, I kept hearing the same scripture.

'It's not by might, nor by power, but by my Spirit saith the Lord.' I've heard it repeatedly from a variety of preachers. In fact, it has happened so often, I wouldn't be surprised if Joyce Meyer were to stop in the middle of her teaching, point at me and quote it."

The woman looked at me as if I was a real nut case. The conversation ended.

Joyce began teaching on a scripture about people not receiving us and quoted that we were to "shake the dust off our feet" when that occurred. All of a sudden, right smack in the middle of her presentation she stopped, seemingly changing direction.

"Wait a minute! Wait a minute! I'm hearing something from the Lord. It has nothing to do with this teaching. '*IT'S NOT BY MIGHT, NOR BY POWER, BUT BY MY SPIRIT SAYS THE LORD!*' That's for someone out there," she said as she pointed in my direction. "You know who you are!"

The woman next to me turned and looked at me, her face riddled with shock and disbelief. I was busy attempting to recover.

The next morning, Lynn mentioned that all of Randy's stuff needed to be moved to the garage. I volunteered. As I was moving all of his belongings, my conscience was pricked.

"Lord, I don't understand this. You hate divorce. You sent me here. I don't understand why I would be helping to throw a man out of his own home and help a couple split up. It's against your will."

No answer. I kept taking things out and placing them in the garage. The final act consisted of Lynn and me lugging a couch down several stairs and shoving the heavy object in the only space left.

Randy was scheduled to show up on Saturday morning. Lynn was visibly nervous as to his upcoming reaction. I asked if she would prefer that I make myself scarce when he arrived. I thought they might want time alone. She began to cry and begged me not to leave. She was afraid. I promised to stay.

Randy arrived. He had been drinking, as usual. It was rather anticlimactic, actually. Shocked by the sight of all of his belongings having been moved to the garage, reality hit him. I literally saw it register on his face. His behavior had resulted in him finally passing the threshold of no return.

He greeted me cordially. We had only met once before, soon after their wedding. Although seemingly somewhat embarrassed by the situation, he posed no threat. After an initial bit of uncomfortable verbal exchange with his soon to be ex-wife, he staggered to the garage and plopped down on the couch. His brother was scheduled to arrive the following day to take his belongings back to their family farm.

Lynn needed something from the garage, but was afraid that if she went to get it, it would lead to an unpleasant scene.

"Do you mind going out there?"

I knocked gently on the side door entrance, announcing that I needed to come in for a minute. Randy looked up from his half-empty beer can and raised it in a mock toast. Deep compassion arose from within me. Although the break-up was clearly his fault, I felt sorry for him. I also felt the Lord prompting me to talk to him--to not simply retrieve the item and scurry out, but to stop and engage him in conversation.

"I'm sorry Randy."

"It's okay. It's my fault. I'm a drunk. She just can't take it anymore. I don't blame her."

"Do you mind if I ask you a question?"

"Nah, I don't mind." He took another sip.

"Why did you start drinking in the first place? How did it get so out of control?"

"Well, it happened when I was in Vietnam. We went out on a mission and my whole company was blown up in front of me. I was the only survivor. I couldn't take it, witnessing my buddies dying like that; all of them--gone. I just can't get past it. Why didn't I die with them?"

"The question you need to be asking, Randy, is not 'why didn't I die with them' but 'why am I still here?' As long as you are breathing it means God still has a purpose for your life. I lost my daughter, three of my best friends and my husband in the space of a year and ten months. Not trying to undermine the relationship you had with your buddies, but my losses hit extremely hard and close to home. It was the most difficult time in my life. I thought I would never recover, but finally, after grieving and allowing the Holy Spirit to work, I learned three extremely important things. God is Sovereign, God is Faithful, and I can trust Him implicitly. I don't have to understand. I wasn't the one who died. I was left here. There is a purpose for me being here. I've come very close to death--numerous times, but God saw to it that I was spared. There is a reason why I was spared, and there is a reason you were spared. I feel like I'm supposed to sing you a song and pray for you. Would you mind?"

"No, go ahead."

I sang a song written by Dottie Rambo; its lyrics penned to the famous tune, *"Danny Boy."*

He Looked Beyond My Fault and Saw My Need:

Amazing grace shall always be my song of praise for it was grace that bought my liberty,

I do not know just why He came to love me so; He looked beyond my fault and saw my need.

I shall forever lift mine eyes to Calvary, to view the cross where Jesus died for me; how marvelous the grace that caught my falling soul...

He looked beyond my fault and saw my need.

Visibly moved by the words in the song, he bowed his head as I prayed for him, thanking me afterward for the prayer and the song. I left the garage. Randy stayed the night in the garage.

The following morning I prepared to leave. Randy was in the kitchen drinking coffee, awaiting his brother's arrival. Lynn greeted me warmly, gave me a hug and thanked me. She asked if I was sure I didn't want her to buy me any perfume. Once again, I said no. She insisted I take $120 for gas, since I had traveled a long way and had staged her entire house. I accepted the gas money. Randy helped guide me, using an atlas to show me the best route back home.

The day after I returned to Tennessee, I stopped to visit Harry, a good friend of mine. He wanted to hear all about my trip. While I was filling him in on the details, his daughter Donna, also a good friend, interrupted.

"Pamela, do you need some perfume? I have two bottles that are brand new and I will never use them."

I was taken aback. Her question came seemingly out of nowhere. Perfume had not been mentioned.

"Sure."

She ran upstairs and came back with the largest size made of Elizabeth Taylor's *Passion,* and an equally large bottle of *Dark Vanilla* by Victoria's Secret. I couldn't believe it! My two favorites! It also dawned on me that this was why I was led by the Lord to say no twice to Lynn's generous offer to buy me perfume.

The following Sunday, I was preparing to leave for church.

"Lord, I need some money."

I have no idea why I said that; it just came out. I was baffled by my statement.

Church was great. I was happy to be back. After the service, the Lord spoke to me in the car.

"Go to Steve* and Sarah's* house," He said.

"But Lord! It's Sunday afternoon, they take naps. You know they have a lot of kids!"

I tried killing some time, riding around town, circling back and almost disobeyed. Once again, I fought His command with my logic and reasoning.

"Lord, I don't want to go there. I haven't even seen them in almost a year! I don't like to disturb couples and their families on Sunday."

"Go there; Now!"

I pulled into their driveway, slowly approached the door, and rang the bell. I heard voices--questioning, wondering, and then sounds of feet scrambling. 'They have eight children!' I thought before God. 'This interruption cannot be welcomed.'

Steve answered the door. He seemed dumbfounded. He was shaking his head in wonder and surprise.

"Wha…? Wha...?" he stammered. "What are you doing here? We haven't seen you in almost a year! Never mind. I know why."

He smiled and ushered me in.

"You do?" I said, surprised by his admission. *I* didn't even know why I was there. How could *he* know?

Sarah peeked around the door--equally surprised, she echoed his sentiments.

"We haven't seen you in forever!"

I sat down and said that the only thing out of the ordinary was a recent trip I had taken to Ft. Worth, Texas. I began telling them about it. Several sentences into my story, Steve interrupted.

"How do you spell your last name?"

"Shut up! I'm in the middle of my story!"

"Seriously, how do you spell it?"

"Why? Why do you need to know that? What does it have to do with my story?"

Sarah interjected. "It looks like he's writing a check."

"A check? Why would you be writing a check to me?"

"Here," he handed me a check, then began explaining his action.

"We all laid down to take a nap. I was just drifting off to sleep when the Lord spoke to me. He said that He was sending someone to my door in a few minutes. I was to give the person $2,000. Within a few minutes, the doorbell rang and there you stood. I knew He meant you. We hadn't seen you in almost a year. I knew He was the reason you were here."

Sarah smiled. If it is the Lord, she's happy.

I was stunned. I hadn't known why I had made the statement that morning about needing money. I hadn't known why the Lord sent me to their house. Now, I didn't know why I had received $2,000 from Him through Steve. As the months went by, the money went to several different people, all with varying needs. The Lord gave explicit instructions as to what amounts went to whom and for what purpose. It was fun; it was amazing, and it was wonderful to be used as His money dispenser.

A few months later, my mother called. She said she had received a call from Lynn's mother. Lynn was distraught and was suffering from depression.

"Why is she depressed?" I asked.

"Well, her husband Randy died."

"No way!" But I was just there a few months ago! What happened?"

"I don't know. You should call and talk to her."

This was shocking news. Scenes from my trip began playing in my mind. 'I hope nothing I did served as a catalyst, Lord.' The unthinkable registered momentarily. 'I hope he didn't commit suicide,' I thought, as I dialed her number. I had no idea what to say.

"Hello?"

"Lynn, it's me. Mom told me the news. I can't believe it. What happened?"

"I can't believe you called. I've been devastated. It's been so bad I had to see a counselor and believe it or not, I was talking about you to her today!"

"What were you saying about me?"I questioned, bracing myself, afraid of her answer.

"I was telling her how you served as a catalyst."

'Oh, no,' I thought.

"How?" I asked.

"You have no idea what happened after you left," she began."Randy's brother and mother showed up. They managed to load all of his stuff into a truck and took him back to their farm. Randy went to his bedroom and locked the door. He wouldn't let anyone in. He wouldn't eat anything. He wouldn't talk. They were afraid of what he might do, or what he had done. Four days later, he emerged from the bedroom. He went to everyone he could think of who he had hurt in his lifetime and repented profusely and then asked for their forgiveness--including his mother, his children and my mother. Then he called me and asked me to take him back. I said, 'I don't even know if I love you anymore, Randy.' He said, 'You do. I know.' I said, 'How do you know that?' Then he said, 'God told me.' As soon as he said that, I knew something dramatic had taken place."

Lynn shared that at the end of the four days, while lying in his bed, he had lifted his hands to God and cried out, "Jesus save me." That's when the transformation had taken place.

"He came to Ft. Worth. He was a changed man. It was like we were on our honeymoon. He couldn't do enough for me. I fell down the stairs and broke my ankle. He waited on me hand and foot. Then, one day I looked at him and said, 'Randy, you look terrible! You need to see a doctor as soon as possible'!"

Randy wanted to go to the doctor in his hometown. He trusted his family physician. Once again, his mother and brother came and picked him up and took him to the hospital. Just before they wheeled him in for exploratory surgery, he told them all that he loved them. He died in the operating room. Unbeknownst to Randy, his body was riddled with metastasized cancer. The alcohol had masked the pain and the disease.

"So, why do you need counseling?"

"Because after ten years of hell, I finally got the husband of my dreams--and then he died!"

I promised to pray for her, but mostly I was overcome, overwhelmed by God's great love for Randy. I asked to go to work for the Lord. His response was to send me all the way from Tennessee to a garage in Ft. Worth, Texas to share His message to one of His children. One of His children whom only He had known was dying and who received His offer of eternal life.

GET THEE OUT OF THY COUNTRY

I had been working for Jesus a few years when the first dream about the Northeast came. I saw myself driving on I-95 through Connecticut. I remember passing a sign that said Stamford. I also had dreams of driving on I-91 and I-93. The routes were completely foreign to me, and I had never heard of the city I had seen. I looked at an atlas. All the routes were located in the northeast. The dreams continued for two years. I saw people I would later meet and whom would play a significant role in the evangelism I was being called to do in this new field.

Having mentioned the fact that each assignment or trip would include a theme scripture, the ones used throughout what has now proven to be a 14 year calling (so far--only God knows how long it will really be) were intriguing. The first one was a passage telling of Jesus' command to the disciples recorded in Luke chapter 10.

"*The Lord now chose seventy-two other disciples and sent them ahead in pairs to all the towns and places he planned to visit. [2] These were his instructions to them: "The harvest is great, but the workers are few. So pray to the Lord who is in charge of the harvest; ask him to send more workers into his fields. [3] Now go, and remember that I am sending you out as lambs among wolves. [4] Don't take any money with you, nor a traveler's bag, nor an extra pair of sandals. And don't stop to greet anyone on the road.*

[5] "Whenever you enter someone's home, first say, 'May God's peace be on this house.' [6] If those who live there are peaceful, the blessing will stand; if they are not, the blessing will return to you. [7] Don't move around from home to home. Stay in one place, eating and drinking what they provide. Don't hesitate to accept hospitality, because those who work deserve their pay.

[8] "If you enter a town and it welcomes you, eat whatever is set before you. [9] Heal the sick, and tell them, 'The Kingdom of God is near you now.' [10] But if a town refuses to welcome you, go out into its streets and say, [11] 'We wipe even the dust of your town from our feet to show that we have abandoned you to your fate. And know this—the Kingdom of God is near!' [12] I assure you; even wicked Sodom will be better off than such a town on judgment day." (NLT)

The other theme scripture given time and again to me was from the Old Testament, Genesis chapter 12.

Vs. 1) Now the LORD had said unto Abram, Get thee out of thy country, and from thy kindred, and from thy father's house, unto a land that I will shew thee:
Gen 12:2 And I will make of thee a great nation, and I will bless thee, and make thy name great; and thou shalt be a blessing:

It is also recorded in the famous "Faith Chapter:"
Hebrews 11.

By faith Abraham, when he was called to go out into a
place which he should after receive for an inheritance,
obeyed; and he went out, not knowing whither he
went.(Verse 8).

As was the case with my first trip, I inquired of the
Lord.

'When will I go?' It was early fall of 2000.

"I will tell you."

At the end of October, He spoke.

"Go."

I packed my car. I didn't know if I was going for a
week, a month, a year or 10 years. All I knew was that I
was to head to Connecticut and at some point He would tell
me where to stop. After leaving my home in Tennessee, I
stopped to stay a weekend in Virginia with a friend; while
there, I visited a local church where I received prayer for
God's will to be done on my trip and for guidance and
protection.

For two years, I had seen the same man in prophetic
dreams of the trip. He was tall, and had dark hair and
brown eyes. Through the duration of the dreams, I saw my
relationship with him evolve. One particular piece of
clothing he wore stood out in the dreams. It was a multi-
colored nylon windbreaker.

Leaving Virginia, I traveled up I-95 and stopped in Nassau, Long Island. I had been told by the Lord to attend the second and so far, the final conference I would attend which featured Joyce Meyer. It had been years since I had attended the one in Ft. Worth.

"I have accommodations for you," The Lord said.

During intermission, a woman overheard a conversation I was having in which I shared that I had come up from Tennessee.

"You're from Tennessee? I can't believe this. The Lord was talking to me about meeting someone from Tennessee today!"

I thought, 'That's cool. I wonder what He was saying about me.'

"Are you staying over? Do you have accommodations? Do you know anyone locally?"

I explained my call by God to the northeast. I told her I had left and traveled solely by faith--trusting Him to guide me. I could see her struggling. She as much as admitted that she was in a quandary, feeling as though the Lord had told her to put me up for the night--yet not trusting Him enough to follow through. I was a total stranger. It would require a leap of faith, one which ultimately, she was unwilling to take. She hung her head and mumbled about how she wished her friend who would have been willing to welcome me into her home had not been out of town.

I was quite disheartened. The woman's disobedience had disrupted the chain of events and the timing of my trip. Rather than leaving bright and early in the morning, I was passing through Stamford late at night. I was rather befuddled as to where to go, what to do. I pulled into the parking lot of a hotel, went in, and was flabbergasted when told the price of a room. I returned to my car and prayed for direction and then continued driving north, up the interstate. It was getting very late; I exited off the highway in the city of Bridgeport and pulled over in a small parking lot smack in the middle of a triangle in the road.

Almost as soon as I had pulled over, seemingly out of nowhere, an older man approached my car and asked if I needed help. I told him that what I was going to tell him would sound strange, but I didn't know what else to do but tell him the truth about my situation. I was called by God as an evangelist to Connecticut; the timing had been thrown off and I didn't know which way to turn.

He looked at me earnestly, concerned.

"You don't want to stay here! Continue driving north. Go to Milford."

He recommended a room at a clean, safe, reasonable motel and gave me explicit directions as to how to get there. I heeded his advice. Later on, once I was tucked safely in for the night, I called several friends in Tennessee and explained my situation. I asked for prayer. Despite the situation, I slept well and had peace.

The following morning, I went to the front desk and turned in my key. Several guests had gathered and were enjoying a Continental breakfast. I was welcomed, offered food and much needed help. One customer was a salesman who rented his room by the month. He offered me his newspaper and suggested that I do as others who travel to the state--inquire about renting a room by the week or month. He showed me a couple of ads and offered me some coins to use the phone.

All my needs were being supplied by total strangers, strangers who were full of mercy and help. I was especially thankful for the stranger who had led me there the night before.

My attention now turned to securing housing in some form. Since I had not been told what the length of my stay would be, renting a room by the week seemed the most viable option.

"Hello?" the man on the other end of the line sounded agitated.

"I'm calling about your ad for a room for rent."

"Listen; can you call me back in about 15 minutes? I have someone on the other line."

I didn't want to call him back. It was going to cost more money to do so, and I just wanted to set up a time to meet with him, but I grudgingly agreed. After all, there were only two ads for a room.

Fifteen minutes later, he answered.

"Hello?"

"I called before--about a room?"

"Yeah, well, what's your name?"

He sounded like a very disgruntled, angry man.

I told him my name, and then was immediately blasted with a tirade about a woman with the same first name who had just been evicted from his home and who had destroyed the place.

I explained that I was neat, paid my bills and was no relation TO THE WOMAN WITH THE SAME FIRST NAME!

A multitude of questions followed. "What do you do for a living? What kind of car do you drive? How old are you? Etc, etc." I felt like I was applying for a position with the National Security Administration.

I asked why he wanted to know so much. His questions seemed awfully invasive and unnecessary.

"I don't let just anybody rent a room!"

"Can't I just see it, and then we can talk?"

Finally a time was set, noon. I also called about the other room advertised, which I would not be able to see until 5 p.m. There were no other ads.

I pulled into the parking lot across the street from the address given. I saw a tall, dark-haired man barking orders. I hung my head.

"Oh, God! Please don't let that be it, and don't let that be him!"

"That's it, and that's him."

Upon closer examination, I realized I was staring at the man I had seen for two years in my dreams.

The guy crossed the road and approached my car.

"You're here about the room?" I nodded.

"Follow me, but the room is a real mess. You probably won't want it."

I followed him up two flights of steps to the second floor of the large Victorian home. We went through several rooms, all of which had been left in a terrible mess. Trash was strewn, covering the floors everywhere I looked. It was disgusting! I shook my head and looked up at him.

"I don't believe I'll take it."

"I didn't think so."

I glanced at my watch. It was just past noon. I could not see the room available at the other location until 5 p.m. For some reason, my heart when out to the man standing before me. As soon as we met, I felt the most incredible *agapé* love for him (the highest form of spiritual love, not carnal, not brotherly). It was very strange and unexpected. I was not the least bit attracted to this man, but I would've given my life for him right then and there.

"I have five hours to kill; why don't I help you clean up this mess? I have nothing else to do; I know absolutely no one in this city, and I don't mind." I added, "Free of charge."

He smiled broadly."Who are you with? The FBI? The CIA? The IRS?"

I laughed. "No, God sent me here.I would like to help you and I have nothing better to do." I watched as he glanced at my outfit: knee-length black pencil skirt, a vibrant-colored stretch top, black fitted blazer and high heels.

"In that?"

"Yes. I work in high heels all the time. Don't worry about it. Hand me a trash bag and let's get to work."

We worked together as a team for close to five hours. I glanced at my watch.

"I need to go check out that other room."

We went across the street to the donut shop. He handed me his phone and let me call the potential landlord. The landlord said the room was ready to look at. I did not have a GPS at the time. The man, Jim,* asked me the address where I was going.I was hesitant to tell him. Although we had worked together for five hours, I didn't know him, and despite my odd reaction toward him, I said a little prayer under my breath and then told him the address.

He said he knew right where it was. If I wanted, he would drive me down there. I have to admit; I was nervous about it. But something, or rather, "Someone" told me to go with him. After all, I had dreamed about this man for two solid years.

We got in the car and drove to the house. I met with the landlord, who had a thick Polish accent. The room was nice and the price was reasonable. I paid him and then went back to Jim's car. I told him I'd taken the room, that it was nice. He drove me back to my car and went above and beyond the call of duty by having me follow him back down to where he had taken me so that I would get there safely.

"I will be going to church tomorrow morning in the center of town. Afterwards, if you want, I could drop by and work some more on your place with you. Free of charge."

His face lit up.

"Really?"

"Yes. Really. I will come by around noon."

The following day, I arrived when I said I would. I believe he was surprised to see me. I don't think he was accustomed to people doing what they said they would do. I worked with him every day from that day on.

After working with him all afternoon, I drove back to the house where I was staying. I found out that my roommates were four men. The Polish landlord stopped by the following morning.

"Eet ees good to have woman in house," he spoke with a thick accent and broken English. "The men be neat. Clean house!" He smiled.

When I arrived in Connecticut, the Lord told me not to be a "Bible thumper," that my time there would be, in essence, a covert operation.

The following week, I worked with Jim every day. Sunday arrived and I went to church.Monday morning my landlord showed up again.

He raised his eyebrows.

"You Chreestian (Christian) woman?"

"Yes."

"I think so. Where you go church?"

"Well, since arriving in Connecticut, I have been going to a Methodist church in town. In Tennessee, I have been a long-time member of a charismatic Baptist Church." I was attending the local Methodist Church in Connecticut because it was close. I knew how to get there and how to get back to the house where I was staying.

"You no go Methodist church! You go Chreestian church!" he insisted, seemingly disturbed by my answer.

The last I heard the Methodists were Christian. I looked at him quizzically, not understanding what he wanted from me.

"Where do you go to church?" I questioned.

"I go Catholic church. You go Chreestian church! I show you. Get in van." He noticed my hesitation.

"I OK. Not worry."

Once again, I found myself wondering before God. 'Lord, should I go with this guy?' I didn't know him at all, but he was adamant about showing me where he thought I should go.

"You come with me now in van. I show you."

I got in his van. Ironically, we landed somewhat near the area where I had been working with Jim. We pulled up to an elaborately constructed building and stayed seated in the van. I stared through the glass doors. An enormous crystal chandelier hung in the foyer. A very expensive, lavish former Italian restaurant had been converted into a non-denominational church.

"You go theeese church!" he ordered.

"But I thought you were Catholic?"

"I am good Catholic! I go every week! You go theese church!"

I shook my head, baffled by his insistence.

"OK. I'll try this church."

He smiled; he was very pleased. We drove back to the house.

I kept my word and began attending there. The people were friendly. The Pastor was a gifted speaker. It was a church similar to those I had attended in Tennessee and other states.

One of the Deacons approached me; we talked at length. I told him that I had come up to the northeast from Tennessee in response to God's apostolic call for me to do the work of an evangelist. He laughed at my story about the landlord having told me to come to their church and asked if my landlord attended there. I said no; he had never attended there himself but had insisted that I did!

It was very different living with roommates. I had never had a roommate before, and now my first experience happened to be living in a house occupied by four men! Two men lived on the first floor. One man lived in the basement. My room was on the second floor, another man had a room across from mine. The men would smile shyly when we would cross paths. We usually did not speak other than an occasional hello. The youngest man had a room on the first floor, near the front door. I saw him the most. One day, he invited me to come into his room for a cup of coffee. He noticed my apprehension.

"Don't worry. I will leave the door open."

I felt prompted by the Lord to accept his invitation. Rock music was blaring in the background. I winced at the sound coming from the large boom box in the corner. He invited me to sit down in a chair next to his desk and poured my coffee. He poured himself a cup and sat down in front of the desk.

He asked me to tell him a little bit about myself--if I didn't mind. I asked him a few questions; we exchanged small talk. I wondered why he was living in that house with the other men. He mentioned that he was recently separated from his wife. I would guess his age as somewhere in his twenties.

Several minutes later, he got up from the desk and began pacing the room. He had been relating the circumstances surrounding his current living conditions and the situation regarding his little boy when suddenly, his face turned beet red as he began talking about his in-laws and his estranged wife, and their role in his not having seen his little boy.

He said his in-laws had caused most of the problems between him and his wife, and rather than standing with him, his wife had taken their side. He had not seen his son in months. His anger quickly escalated and turned into rage. I watched him grow increasingly agitated as he spoke.

A scripture began floating in my mind; "Out of the abundance of the heart the mouth speaks."

"I'm going to show them! I have it all planned!" He seethed. "I'm going to kill all of them and then get my boy!"

I was taken aback by his words yet not fearful, which didn't make sense given the circumstances. I didn't know how to respond. A quick prayer arose inside of me. I asked Jesus for help. 'What do I do? What can I say?'

Calm settled over me as the words poured out...

"Well Ray, if what you say is true, and you really plan on wiping out your wife and her entire family, one of two things is getting ready to happen."

I had his attention.

"One, you are getting ready to go to prison and get fried, or, you will go to prison for life-- in which case your son will be an orphan and farmed out to foster homes. In all likelihood, he will be abused all his life or never loved like he would have been by his parents or family members. Naturally, they would not be available because you would have killed his mother and any family members who could have taken care of him, and *you* obviously couldn't take care of him because, as I said, you will either be dead or in prison for life."

Reality set in; he sat down and hung his head.

"Ray, have you ever attended a church?"

"No."

"Never?"

"No; never."

"Well, I'm a Christian. Would you mind if I said a prayer for you?"

"No. I don't mind."

He bowed his head. The rock music continued to blare in the background. I asked the Lord to take control of the situation and give Ray peace. I prayed for everyone involved and for reconciliation. I prayed for Ray to have a calm spirit and for him to be able to see his little boy and that no evil would befall any of the family members. I looked up. Ray smiled and looked embarrassed or possibly ashamed of the behavior he had displayed only minutes before. He thanked me as I rose to leave.

"Want to come to church with me this Sunday?" I asked, hopeful.

"OK."

Ray did indeed go to church with me that following Sunday…and several times after that. The first Sunday, as we were traveling, Ray pointed to a ditch.

"That's where I was going to bury them."

I nodded and said I was glad that his plans had now changed. I found out why Jesus used my landlord to make me attend that particular church. They were blessed with a very active, on-fire men's ministry. I spoke with the Deacon who had befriended me and told him about Ray. They agreed to come over and minister to him. They poured into him. Many of the men shared openly, revealing their own past struggles with anger, bitterness and the inability to forgive. They picked him up and took him to their Bible study. They loved him into the fold.

I had gone away for a few months. When I stopped by to visit my former roommates, I happened to notice that Ray's room was empty.

"Oh, he doesn't live here anymore." Ron said.

"Really? Why?"

"He and his wife reconciled. He stopped by a couple months ago with his son, cute little boy. They are really happy."

I thanked the Lord for sending me to help thwart what would have been a deadly, devastating situation. It didn't seem plausible that I had not experienced fear in the face of such a potentially volatile situation.

What I do know is that God loves everyone, and no one is beyond His grasp, His redemptive power. Nevertheless, I had been baffled by Ray's transformation; I shouldn't have been however. With man, this is impossible, but with God-all things are possible.

Isa 6:8 Also I heard the voice of the Lord, saying, Whom shall I send, and who will go for us? Then said I, Here am I; send me.

TO BE (LIEVE) or NOT TO BE (LIEVE)

THAT IS THE QUESTION

It is quite the sad state of affairs when a term actually used to describe Christians isn't really accurate. I am addressing the term "Believers." Granted, on some level we are believers. We believe in Jesus, but how far exactly does our range of belief extend?

I have come to the conclusion that many members of the modern day church have very little faith, very little belief. The church has become increasingly secular; the temptation to trust in the arm of the flesh has superseded the Word of God. Unfortunately, it is not a new phenomenon. Jesus met with the same problem out of "believers" (ahem) when he walked the earth, and He is God. Take a look at a few examples below:

Matthew 13:58 And he did not many mighty works there because of their unbelief.

Matthew 17:20 And Jesus said unto them, Because of your unbelief: for verily I say unto you, If ye have faith as a grain of mustard seed, ye shall say unto this mountain, Remove hence to yonder place; and it shall remove; and nothing shall be impossible unto you.

Mark 6:6 And he marveled because of their unbelief. And he went round about the villages, teaching.

Mark_9:24 And straightway the father of the child cried out, and said with tears, Lord, I believe; help thou mine unbelief.

Mark_16:14 Afterward he appeared unto the eleven as they sat at meat, and upbraided them with their unbelief and hardness of heart, because they believed not them which had seen him after he was risen.

I addressed this topic somewhat in my story "Miracles (Part 2)" in my book, *Life Lessons Book One.* Somewhere along the line, I had hopped on board the unbelieving train. Oh, I *acted* as though I thought all things were possible. I professed belief that I had the power to move mountains, but when faced with one of the most miraculous events of my life, suddenly, I became aware of having fallen *WAY* short of the description of myself as a "believer."

My however-many-ton vehicle and I were miraculously transported by God out of the totally boxed-in fast lane on the Dallas North Central Expressway and placed on a non-existent exit ramp. Oh yeah. It was not a typical day!

I won't rehearse the complete details, (You can order Book One and read them), however, the interesting part happened after people had read the story in my book, or heard me relate the story publicly.

First, I had been in a Wednesday evening church service. The Pastor had been going through the book of Acts. On that night he was teaching about Philip the evangelist who had baptized an Ethiopian Eunuch. He read from Acts Chapter 8:

Acts 8:26 And the angel of the Lord spake unto Philip, saying, Arise, and go toward the south unto the way that goeth down from Jerusalem unto Gaza, which is desert.

Acts 8:29 Then the Spirit said unto Philip, Go near, and join thyself to this chariot.

Acts 8:30 And Philip ran thither to him, and heard him read the prophet Esaias, and said, Understandest thou what thou readest?

Acts 8:31 And he said, How can I, except some man should guide me? And he desired Philip that he would come up and sit with him.

Acts 8:34 And the eunuch answered Philip, and said, I pray thee, of whom speaketh the prophet this? of himself, or of some other man?

Acts 8:35 Then Philip opened his mouth, and began at the same scripture, and preached unto him Jesus.

Acts 8:37 And Philip said, If thou believest with all thine heart, thou mayest. And he answered and said, I believe that Jesus Christ is the Son of God.

Acts 8:38 And he commanded the chariot to stand still: and they went down both into the water, both Philip and the eunuch; and he baptized him.

Acts 8:39 And when they were come up out of the water, the Spirit of the Lord caught away Philip, that the eunuch saw him no more: and he went on his way rejoicing.

Act_8:40 But Philip was found at Azotus: and passing through he preached in all the cities, till he came to Caesarea.

So, the kicker of the story is found in verse 40. Apparently Philip, (rather than Scotty of Star Trek fame), had been beamed up, landing in Azotus through what has been termed supernatural transportation.

As was the case at every Wednesday service, the Pastor asked if anyone had any comments about what we had just studied. I raised my hand.

"That happened to me."

"What happened to you?"

"I was miraculously transported also--like Philip."

"Why don't you come up and tell us about it," he said.

I walked to the front of the church and shared what had been the greatest miracle I had witnessed since becoming a Christian. Afterward, the Pastor openly repented for placing boundaries on God.

Faith is never stationary. It is either increasing or decreasing. We often don't even realize that is has been "leaking out."

The other interesting response was from ordinary people like me. My story had afforded them the opportunity to tell of their own similar miraculous experiences, ones they finally felt comfortable sharing. One person had much the same experience as I had; only his had occurred in Britain. The other one had an even more dramatic deliverance! I wonder how many of us have tales which we are hesitant to share even amongst "believers," because we know beforehand or at least suspect, that they wouldn't believe our accounts?

This brings me to the definition of God. By definition, God is a supreme being for whom nothing is impossible. If it were, he would not be God. If anything was impossible for God, He would be impotent (without power) rather than omnipotent (all-powerful).

Granted, He *has* placed some conditions on us, such as, "only believe," and, "if you have faith," etc.

Jesus told us that these signs would follow all BELIEVERS: we would lay hands on the sick and they would recover, in His name we would cast out devils, speak with new tongues, etc., before and *AFTER HE WAS RESURRECTED.*

In the book of Acts, people were healed by the mere shadow of a disciple walking past. Why aren't we doing these things? The answer is simple, yet disturbing. We have become Believers who don't believe.

As I shared before, I was widowed, but when (what would become) my husband and I were on our first date, he glanced over at me briefly while we were on our way to Fall Creek Falls and posed a question.

"What do you think it takes to have a good relationship?"

"Well, I believe it is very important that the couple have a similar socio-economic background, as well as religious leanings, and even agree politically for the most part."

"It's either there, or it ain't." He smiled.

I understood.

Belief. It's either there or it ain't. You are either serving an impotent God, bound by your finite, carnal, limited mind, or you are serving God Almighty, the Supreme Being for whom *NOTHING IS IMPOSSIBLE.*

"I WANT HIS MERCEDES!

I hadn't been working with Jim very long when I revealed that not only was I a Christian, but I was actively involved in ministry, evangelism in particular. I didn't want to tell Jim because the Lord told me my evangelism was to be covert. Remember His admonition to me? I was not to be a, "Bible Thumper." But Jim was constantly grilling me and I finally buckled.

"Holy—!"

"Yeah. That's really why I am here."

"Hommina hommina hommina…. Holy… Jesus, Mary, and Joseph!"

His response was quite comical. I gathered that he was rather unaccustomed to hanging with people involved in the ministry. He determined to tone down his cussing. That never happened in all the years I was around him. He used expletives as nouns, subjects, predicates, adjectives, adverbs, any way he could fit them in. One day, just after he let loose with a tirade consisting of several sentences filled with his cursing, a man knocked on the door. Although I was standing behind Jim, I could still be seen.

It was one of his tenants.

"Man, I'm sorry I'm a couple days late on the rent. I don't know how the hell I forgot."

Jim let loose with a self-righteous admonishment of his tenant, raking him over the coals for using the word hell.

"Hey! Watch your big mouth! You should know better than to use that kind of language in front of a woman!"

I rolled my eyes at him as soon as the door was closed.

"What a hypocrite!" I said.

"What?"

He really didn't know what I was talking about!

After my "calling" sunk in, Jim actually began to revel in it. He introduced me to friends and family.

"Get this! You won't believe what she is!"

Response from family and friends was always similar to his.

"HOLY—!" fill in the expletive.

Jim took me to see his mother who was in a nursing home. She had called and told him she was very sick. I told Jim that I often prayed for people who were sick and that I had witnessed some truly miraculous recoveries over a span of many years. That was the case with his mother. The Lord healed her numerous times during the course of our friendship.

One day, he approached me with an unusual request.

"Hey, a friend of mine went to the hospital for tests and the news wasn't good. I told him about you, that you pray for people. Would you mind talking to him if I call him? I think he would like prayer. He's pretty concerned."

"Not at all."

He pulled out his cell phone and scrolled down to Rick's number.

"Hey Rick, I've got her right here. Want to talk to her?"

"Hello?" I said.

"Hello. Jim says you pray for people."

"I do. I've seen God do a lot of miracles through the years. He told us to pray one for another--that you may be healed. Why are you in need of prayer?"

"Well, I guess it couldn't hurt. I went to the hospital. They ran tests. It shows I have nodules."

Rick is Catholic.

"Well, would you like me to come over and anoint you with oil and pray for you in person, or would you rather I pray for you over the phone?"

"OVER THE PHONE!"

I realized very quickly that the thought of me praying for him in person was very scary to Rick, despite his deep concern regarding the test results. His fears were based on his lifestyle and were definitely founded. He had been a chain smoker most of his life. He knew the risks. I knew he had the "C" word on his mind.

"Ok. Ready?" I prayed for the nodules to disappear. I prayed for fear to leave him. He thanked me and said they wanted him to come back soon for more tests. He would let me know how things turned out.

Jim seemed pleased. He had done something noble. His smile was one of satisfaction, a deed well done. I smiled back. It was pretty cute.

Several days later, Rick called Jim and asked to speak to me.

"I went back and guess what? The nodules are gone!" He was a believer.

Soon after the good news, I traveled back down to Tennessee for a couple of months. It was good to have a rest. Then the Lord sent me back up.

I stopped by to see Jim. He was very glad to see me. He knew it meant free help. A few days later, he wanted to talk to me about something he said was important.

"I heard from Rick. He had more tests done. He asked if you were in town."

"He wants to talk to me?"

"Yes, as soon as possible."

He grabbed his cell and called Rick.

"Hey! Guess who's standing here?" Some small talk and laughter was exchanged before he handed me the phone.

"Hi Rick. Jim said you wanted to talk to me?"

"Well, I had some more tests done and the nodules are gone-- but they found a spot, actually, more than one, on both of my lungs."

"Oh. I will keep you in prayer then."

"Thanks."

A few days later, the Lord spoke to me.

"I want you to wash Rick's feet, anoint him with oil, pray for him and sing him a song."

I needed to use Jim's house to do what the Lord asked, and I knew that might present a problem. First of all, it was the northeast; foot-washings weren't commonplace, and I cringed at the thought of Jim's reaction. I had not been accustomed to the practice either, until I attended some Pentecostal churches in Tennessee (mostly on New Year's Eve) and later, on Maundy Thursday in some Methodist churches. There were a few other times it occurred at some Ladies Bible studies, but it was still somewhat of a rare practice.

"Are you crazy????? NO WAY! He'll think you're a nut!" Jim's reaction was not a surprise; nevertheless, it was very disappointing.

"So?"

"NO! You are not going to wash his feet here! And, he will get the wrong idea!"

"But I need to obey God. There's a reason why He has told me to do it. Trust me, it wasn't my idea-- but when the Lord tells me to do something, I need to do it."

This was going to be difficult. I was in a quandary. I prayed. Soon afterward, Jim came over to me.

"I need to obey God, Jim."

By this time, his focus had turned to washing his car. I had already called Rick and told him I would pray for him, but I had not mentioned what the Lord had told me to do.

"Do whatever you have to do," Jim said, disgusted, as he headed toward the door. "I don't know why you pray for him anyway. He still smokes the stupid—! I hope he croaks. His wife will sell me his Mercedes cheap."

Rick drove up soon afterward. I asked him to sit on the couch.

"Uh, Rick. I know this is going to sound odd. I'm sure it's a practice that you are not accustomed to, but the Lord told me to wash your feet, anoint you with oil, pray for you and sing you a song."

Rick raised both hands in the air, lifted his legs up and out, and yelled as he laughed loudly, "I don't care! Wash all of me!" Jim was right.

"No, Rick," I said, disgusted. "I am not going to wash all of you. I'm going to do what The Lord said--nothing else."

Fulfilling what Jesus had asked me to do; I anointed Rick with oil and prayed. The presence of God was so strong; I could barely remain standing as I prepared to sing. I knew Rick could feel His presence as well. It was so thick it manifested as a misty white cloud in the room, tangible evidence.

After I finished the song, Rick rose, thanked me and left. Jim came in a short while later and asked how it went.

"Good."

Several days later, Rick called. His voice was filled with elation.

"The latest tests came back. There was no way to explain it, the doctors said. The spots are gone! My lungs are totally clear!"

The Lord wasn't finished with Rick. Years later, I was in a church service on a Wednesday evening when the Lord interrupted.

"Leave church. Call Rick. Go to his house and pray for him." I hadn't seen or spoken to Rick in years. I called him from my car.

"Hey there, Rick! This is Pamela."

"Well, where have you been? I haven't heard from you in a long time!"

"I went down south, but I've been back up for a while. Listen, the Lord wants me to come to your house and pray for you for some reason. What's going on?"

"I'm headed to Johns Hopkins in the morning. They're going to amputate my leg."

"I'll be right over."

I greeted Rick's wife and explained that the Lord told me to come over to their house to pray for her husband. The familiar stench of cigarette smoke filled the room. Jim's words, spoken years before, filled my thoughts. "He keeps smoking; let him croak! I can get his Mercedes cheap!"

I reached into my purse and felt the small glass vial of anointing oil. My thoughts drifted back to the day I had received the smooth aromatic mixture.

My long-time friend Carol is Cherokee Indian and proud of it.

"I don't like to be called Native American, Pam. I'm an Indian. That's what I am; that's what I like to be called," she told me several times throughout the years.

A lifelong smoker, I heard her distinctive deep, gravelly, slow drawl play in my memory.

"Why Pam, the Lord told me to give you this." She handed me the small vial.

"I know you don't want to hear it but He's givin' you a new gift; the gift of healing. I know how you feel about it, but I have to obey God. He also told me to give you this."

She handed me a small, thin booklet addressing the subject of healing.

Her apologetic demeanor had to do with her understanding of my feelings toward some high-profile television evangelists, many of whom had been exposed as frauds and who *preyed on* widows, rather than *praying for* widows--using their "two mites" to heap lavish abundance on themselves. It left a bad taste in my mouth for anyone begging for money on TV--as it should.

My mind then drifted back to a memory from years before, when I had actually attended a well-known minister's healing conference at the urging of a friend, who felt that I should sing in the choir at the event. Shortly before I was widowed, my husband and I had driven up to a major city in Kentucky. I had to go early for practice before the service began. He dropped me off at the Convention Center and drove back to the motel.

A plump, sequined laden woman, with very highly teased, bleached-blonde hair turned toward me.

"Have you ever been to one of his conferences?"

"No. My friend felt like I should be here. That's the only reason I came."

"Well, I travel everywhere he goes! I haven't missed one! He's wonderful!"

I was very uncomfortable. I wanted out. The choir director went over some songs.

"The last song will be, "To God Be the Glory," he instructed. "When it begins, the lights will go up all over the house and he will walk out on stage."

Sure enough, as we belted out the song, the minister walked out dressed all in white, the lights came on all over the Center. We were still singing "To God Be the Glory" and I was mortified. I thought the minister was going to be eaten by worms, right then and there--just like Herod!

As difficult as it is to believe, the situation worsened. Several other high-profile ministers were on stage. Each one stood, taking the microphone and commending the main minister, not God. After the fifth one rose to praise him, I prayed to the Lord.

"Please God! Help me get out of here without making a scene. I don't want to be a part of this glorification of man!

Please, have them turn down the lights so I can run out of here and never look back!"

"Please watch carefully as we show a short video." The minister announced. The lights went down and I raced out. I called my husband.

"I've been waiting for your call. The Lord told me you weren't going to stay, so I just relaxed in the room and didn't go anywhere. I wanted to be close by so I could pick you up when you called."

My mind finally returned to the present. Rick's wife chose not to join us for the prayer. She left before I began. Ironically, although she had been the daughter of two Christian missionaries, she was not interested in anything to do with religion in any form.

I stood before Rick. The fragrance of the oil permeated the room; it was unlike anything I had smelled before. Every time I used it, the person was healed. I anointed Rick and prayed for a miracle. He smiled and thanked me. I left.

A few days later, he called. The physicians at Johns Hopkins determined there was no need to follow through with the scheduled amputation.

PARTY HEARTY!

The most unusual aspect of my having been called to the northeast had been the types of venues in which I was most often sent to bring the good news of the Gospel. I had been called by God to do the "party circuit."

I know it sounds odd, but if you think about it logically, it makes great sense. Where are people "of the world"? They are out satisfying the desires of the flesh. Where self is God, flesh is all important.

In the south, I had often found myself speaking of Jesus in humble, rural settings, up north I was in a $4.5 million dollar home in Greenwich, CT.

"What do you do Pamela?" the owner enquired.

"Well, I am a minister, an evangelist sent to this area."

"Really?"

I could tell that bit of news had made him terribly uncomfortable. It was not at all what he expected to hear. As I spoke with him, he became more intrigued. Through a "word of knowledge" from the Lord I was able to "read his mail." So much so, he shared that until recently, he had not met any people like me but had actually met a Baptist only a few weeks before who had also spoken to him about Jesus and now it was giving him, "pause," cause to reflect on what it might mean.

The wealthy man worked in New York City. The Baptist had been a business acquaintance from the south who had witnessed to him about salvation. I had apparently come along to drive his point home. One plants, another waters, but it is God who gives the increase.

I went to Christmas gatherings, Jewish holiday celebrations, Kentucky Derby parties, Oscar nights. I was in mansions, on sleek boats, four-story Yachts, at Central Park and on Madison Avenue. I frequented museums, attended plays and symphonies at Yale University and sat in the audience at the American Idol Tour. I witnessed in art galleries, jazz bars, rock concerts, blues festivals and preached in a present-day "speakeasy."

I remembered the accusations against Jesus. "How is it he eats and drinks with publicans and sinners?" The question was asked by Scribes and Pharisees.

One night I will never forget happened on New Year's Eve. I had been invited to a party ushering in the New Year. It was held at a beautiful home. There were hushed conversations in the air when I arrived. Apparently, the daughter of the hosts had said she might show up and their receptivity was mixed. They loved their daughter but she had been a prodigal for several years, having turned to drugs and prostitution on the streets of New York City.

The night had been celebratory. The daughter had shown up and was behaving. Laughter abounded. Around 2 o'clock in the morning, the Lord told me to take her aside. He had a "word" for her. I asked her to step into the den for a moment. I told her I wanted to talk to her about something.

We stood facing each other in front of the crackling fireplace. All of a sudden I began to speak prophetic words to her from the Lord, words of love, not condemnation. The prophecy was detailed and lengthy. The atmosphere of the room changed with His presence. She began weeping with joy and relief. We hugged. The healing of her soul was instantaneous. Jesus had indeed come to her rescue and her life was transformed. She was miraculously delivered from drug addiction and prostitution that very day.

I found that in the south there was something I called, "reverse snobbery." By that I mean, many ministers viewed the wealthy with great disdain. It was seemingly ok to bring the Gospel to the poor and beggarly but not to those who were the 'high and lofty," the well-to-do. I remembered the words of Jesus in Revelation to the Laodiceans, who had this world's wealth.

"And unto the angel of the church of the Laodiceans write; These things saith the Amen, the faithful and true witness, the beginning of the creation of God;

I know thy works, that thou art neither cold nor hot: I would thou wert cold or hot.

So then because thou art lukewarm, and neither cold nor hot, I will spue thee out of my mouth.

Because thou sayest, I am rich, and increased with goods, and have need of nothing; and knowest not that thou art wretched, and miserable, and poor, and blind, and naked:

I counsel thee to buy of me gold tried in the fire, that thou mayest be rich; and white raiment, that thou mayest be clothed, and that the shame of thy nakedness do not appear; and anoint thine eyes with eyesalve, that thou mayest see.

As many as I love, I rebuke and chasten: be zealous therefore, and repent.

Behold, I stand at the door, and knock: if any man hear my voice, and open the door, I will come in to him, and will sup with him, and he with me.

To him that overcometh will I grant to sit with me in my throne, even as I also overcame, and am set down with my Father in his throne.

He that hath an ear, let him hear what the Spirit saith unto the churches. (Rev 3:14-22).

Salvation is needed by all and available to all.

GREATER VISION

I was very disturbed. I had been deeply hurt by something that Jim had done, so much so, that I searched internet ads for rooms/roommates wanted in neighboring states. The situation had served as a catalyst--propelling me to leave what had now become a comfort zone and traveling further up in the northeast, continuing my apostolic/evangelistic trek.

An ad seeking a roommate 30 miles outside of Boston stood out. I quickly responded with an email expressing interest. It was far more reasonable than what I was currently paying in CT. My weekly rent would be due again soon. The plan was to leave before I spent money on another week's rent, money which would be better applied to the rent at the next place. After all, in my dream, I had seen myself traveling not only on I-95, but on I-91 and I-93.

A guy answered. The room was available.

"Come on up."

I drove a few hours, all the while grieved in the very depths of my being because I had left Jim, the man I had been working with for so many months that our lives had become intricately intertwined, the man the Lord had shown me for so long in my prophetic dreams. I doubted that I would ever see him again.

I arrived around noon. The two bedroom apartment was located on the third floor of a Victorian house. I had gone from the comfort of my paid-for home on multiple acres in Tennessee, to an overnight stay at a motel and then to a room in a Boarding house in Connecticut. Now, I would share an apartment with a single guy in Massachusetts. The main areas would be used in common; each of us had our own bedroom.

My roommate would not be back to meet me until later that afternoon. He made prior arrangements with his landlord, who was instructed to accept the month's rent from me and then let me into the apartment. I paid the rent, after which he led me upstairs, unlocked the door and showed me which bedroom would be mine. The only furnishing was a mattress on the floor.

As was the case before, when I had first arrived in Connecticut, I knew no one. I wondered if I had missed the Lord's will. 'Why am I here?' I questioned. I felt disoriented. I had no idea why I was where I was, but I was there now. I had to accept my lot in life. I felt very alone. I lay down and began to nap.

There was a knock on my bedroom door.

"Yes?"

"Hi!" He greeted me with a smile. "I'm your roommate. Since you don't know anyone here, I was wondering if you might want to go with me to a meeting tonight," the young man standing before me was well dressed, clean-cut and very nice.

"What kind of meeting?"

"I'm a member of Alcoholics Anonymous. Have you ever attended a meeting?"

"No."

"Well, since you don't know anyone here, would you like to go with me? It might be interesting."

"Ok."

We went to the meeting and he was right. It *was* interesting. I enjoyed hearing the people's stories, how their lives had changed. I enjoyed witnessing the crowd celebrating the various milestones in their lives--the records they had attained by not succumbing to the temptation of alcohol, having chosen to stop the destruction their addiction had caused in their lives.

After the meeting, my roommate, Darren* asked if I would like to go to his sponsor's house for a bite to eat. He assured me that I would like him and his wife. They knew I had come with him. I was invited to their home even though I was a stranger.

We arrived. I felt very comfortable. I was introduced to the couple, Tom* and Elise* and then seated at the head of the table. Elise sat at the opposite end of the table, directly across from me. The food was welcomed; I was hungry, and the company was pleasant. The lightness of the conversation shifted as they both shared their battles with alcoholism. After Tom related his struggle, I was shocked by what Elise revealed.

When Elise was five years old, she had been brutally raped by her father and brother, incest, the dirty family secret. The years of abuse had taken their toll; Elise had chosen to escape through alcohol, which was destroying her life. When Tom sought help through AA, Elise had followed suit. The alcohol addiction had been dealt with, but Elise was still dealing with an aftermath of bitterness, hatred and the inability to forgive those who had abused her.

"My Psychiatrist said that by not forgiving them, I am literally killing myself. My body is in the process of shutting down even though I am still a young woman. He has tried everything. I just can't do it."

"Your Doctor is a Christian?"

"No. But he said that me choosing to forgive them is the only thing left that can stop me from dying."

I was amazed that a secular psychiatrist had given that kind of advice.

"Elise, choosing to forgive someone doesn't mean that what they did was ok. You would not be sanctioning or condoning their abuse, their behavior, by your act of forgiving them. Forgiveness heals you--not them, although sometimes it does help them heal.

Oftentimes, the people we need to forgive aren't even alive anymore, but we have to do it for ourselves. When we choose not to forgive it hurts us, not them. They are sleeping peacefully at night while our lives are torn apart and we are living in the gall of bitterness. The Bible says it's like a cancer, which not only attacks our bodies and our health, but defiles all those around us. I encourage you to ask God first to give you the *desire* to forgive them, and afterward, to give you the *strength* that will enable you to forgive them."

As I was finishing my thought, Elise screamed out.

"It's HER!"

"What?" Tom asked, surprised by his wife's declaration.

"It's HER, TOM! The woman IN MY VISION! You know--what I told you this morning! It's her!"

"Ohhhhh…" Tom nodded as he remembered their conversation early that morning.

Darren and I looked at each other. Both of us were rather bewildered by what was transpiring between the couple. Finally, Elise explained.

"This morning, soon after I woke up, I saw a vision for the first time in my life. It was a vision of a woman seated at our table talking to me. I told Tom what had happened, what I had seen. I didn't understand why I had the vision but now I know."

Although at the time, Elise did not profess to be a Christian, her inward thoughts tumbled out.

"God sent you. That was why I had the vision."

She broke down.

I was humbled and thanked God for sending me. I no longer wondered why I was there. I counseled her further and made sure she had materials in hand which would help her with the process of forgiving those who had hurt and betrayed her so deeply.

Elise finally chose to forgive. Her decision freed her from the bondage of an emotional prison and gained back her life. Today, she is living out her dream on a beautiful island beach with her husband. She is no longer a slave held by chains of bitterness.

A popular saying sums it up well. "Not forgiving someone is like drinking poison and waiting for the other person to die."

And as for those she forgave…they will answer to a Holy, Righteous, and Just God.

Mat 6:12, 14-15: And forgive us our debts, as we forgive our debtors.

For if ye forgive men their trespasses, your heavenly Father will also forgive you:

But if ye forgive not men their trespasses, neither will your Father forgive your trespasses.

COME BACK!

Darren and I returned to the apartment. The following day he showed me Boston in all its glory. We saw Harvard. We ate at an Indian restaurant and visited various galleries. We witnessed busloads of tourists traveling through the center of the city. The evening culminated in our viewing an off-Broadway style of film noir. The experience was wonderful! It is very different when a native shows you the land than when you are simply a tourist trying to see things on your own. The natives know best.

Despite Jesus having used me to bring His profound emotional healing to a veritable stranger and the incredible time I was having with Darren and my proximity to all the sights and sounds afforded me in the Boston area, my grief over having left Connecticut, and especially Jim, never dissipated. I felt there was grave unfinished business left in regard to him. I finally called.

"Hey. I feel terrible over the way things were when I left."

A short, loving laugh was followed by a tender, hopeful question.

"Want to come back?"

Although I didn't need his permission to return to my call in Connecticut, somehow his question made all the difference. I breathed a sigh of relief and then broke the news to Darren. Even though I had paid for the whole month and had stayed only two days, I didn't ask for any of my money to be returned. It was well worth the cost to help give back life to a woman, sowing a minor monetary seed in her recovery. I left the following morning.

THE GLORY CLOUD

As was experienced during Rick's healing prayer, what I often refer to as the "Glory Cloud" of God's presence continued to show up and still fills the room when "He" is at work.

I remembered back when I was traveling to Connecticut and had stopped to see relatives in Pennsylvania on the way. I shared some of the miraculous things I had seen. When I told them of the instant healings I had witnessed, my cousin asked if I thought he could receive such a healing. I assured Him God is the same--no matter the person, no matter the place. His Healing is available everywhere and for everyone.

He revealed that they had found a tumor on his spine. He was terrified of the surgery which would be required to remove it. Doctors told him there was a very good chance he would lose his ability to walk. His fear was understandable. Who wouldn't be experiencing apprehension at that thought? My young, handsome, vibrant cousin also said that his girlfriend was in need of healing as well. She had been diagnosed as having Hepatitis C, for which there is still no cure.

I brought out the anointing oil, laid hands on them and the Glory Cloud filled the room. They were both healed.

I made it to Connecticut just in time to help Jim with a "Tag Sale." In other areas of the country they are referred to as Garage/Yard sales. While I had gone into his house to find something he wanted brought out to sell, Jim had engaged in conversation outside with a woman who had shown up at his sale. Apparently, she was battling cancer. He shared his own battle with the disease years prior, and then told her about me. He told her to knock on the door and talk with me, that I prayed for people and they were often healed; he had witnessed it.

Not only had he witnessed the healing of his friend Rick, but his own mother had come close to death on several occasions. Each time, we raced to the nursing home where she was living, whereupon I would anoint her with oil and pray. Each time God arrived on the scene, and she was miraculously healed. It was those remembrances which were running through his mind and which caused him to encourage her to come inside and receive prayer.

I opened the door. A tall, thin woman stood before me. She was wearing a vibrant colored scarf layered around her hairless head. I knew she was probably going through Chemotherapy.

"Hi. The man outside said you are a minister. He told me to come inside and talk with you."

"Come on in." I invited her to sit down, and then asked if she was a Christian.

"No." She then revealed that she was sick but never shared the specific diagnosis.

"Well, I'm a Christian and I would be happy to pray for your healing if you would like."

At that moment, her eyes filled with tears as she lifted her hands up high and cried out, "I'll take anything!"

As I anointed her with oil and prayed, once again the "Glory Cloud" filled the room. Her face lit up; she was glowing. I suspected I was glowing also. I had seen the manifestation of God's Holy Spirit many times throughout the years. His presence causes people to glow. I felt a massive love for this stranger; her willingness to receive was very refreshing. She was demonstrating more faith than I had witnessed in many "believers" I had encountered. Many of whom were often hard and suspicious, as well as unbelieving. The contrast of her demeanor with the others struck me as not only ironic, but quite disheartening.

She thanked me for the prayer and left. I never heard from her again.

Jim had a very thin buddy he referred to behind his back as "Skinny Timmy*." Long-time friends, they had been there for each other during hard times throughout the span of their friendship, even though they often went years without contact. Their friendship was characterized by its often sporadic bouts of absences from one another's lives.

Jim had purchased some items at an auction house which he had stored in a large box truck in his driveway. There was a particular item he had wanted me to see. He had mentioned it numerous times. Finally, succumbing to his constant badgering about seeing the item, I stopped by. I approached the back of the truck where Jim was standing and asked to see it.

As he was pulling a large box out of the back of the truck, I was completely overwhelmed by the feeling that something terrible had happened to Skinny Timmy. I mentioned it to Jim. He asked what I thought it was. I didn't know. All I knew was that I was overcome with the urge to pray for him right away, so I did.

The next day was Sunday. I stopped by to say hi to Jim before I went to church, which had become a recent Sunday morning ritual. He invited me in and explained that he hadn't gotten any sleep during the night.

"Why not?"

"I had just gotten to sleep and then, at 3:00 in the morning, Skinny Timmy called. He had collapsed and was taken by ambulance to the hospital yesterday at 5:45 pm."

I remembered having looked at my watch the day before--when I had felt the urgent need to pray for Skinny Timmy. The time had been 5:45 pm.

"Anyway, he needed a ride home from the hospital. He thinks he's gonna croak. He started talking about God and stuff. I didn't know what to say to him, so I invited him over this morning. I want you to talk to him."

"But I'm on my way to church!"

"Well skip it. You need to talk to him about God. I don't know what the H--- to say to him!"

I weighed the situation. Which was more important, my attending a service or a man's salvation? I put my things down on the table and awaited Skinny Timmy's arrival. A few minutes later there was a knock on the door.

The two men greeted each other with an uncomfortable slight hug and slap on the back. Jim told him to sit down. He said I wanted to talk to him. Then he left the room to cook hamburgers while Timmy and I talked.

"What happened? What's going on, Timmy?"

"I was standing at the bus stop and all of a sudden, I collapsed. I thought I was going to die right then and there."

We talked about his past. He had been injured years before in a terrible fall. He almost died. His mother was a strong Christian who had prayed for him and nursed him back to health. He admitted that he needed God. It was time.

I walked him through the prayer of salvation. As he cried and said yes to God, once again the room filled with the Glory of God. Skinny Timmy was lit up; his face was glowing and I could see that his deep concern and fear had been replaced with joy and peace.

Jim came back into the room. He smiled. We ate burgers as the angels in heaven were rejoicing.

Luke 15:10: Likewise, I say unto you, there is joy in the presence of the angels of God over one sinner that repenteth.

WORD OF KNOWLEDGE

In I Corinthians chapter 12, there are nine spiritual gifts listed which we are exhorted to "desire." One of the gifts is the "word of knowledge," often described as supernatural revelation knowledge concerning something in the present. For example, someone might go up to an individual and say, "I believe the Lord is telling me a word for you. He wants you to forgive someone who has hurt you recently. The inability on your part to forgive this individual is keeping you from moving on with what God has for your life. It is keeping you from promotion from above." When something like this takes place, the person can heed the word or disregard it. If you "bear witness" that it truly is from the Lord, it would behoove you to heed it.

I'm describing this gift because it was the very one used to bring me into the lives of a group which, to this day, I am blessed to be a part of and which the Lord has used to carry out several of His agendas.

"Pamela, I was going through the paper and I saw an ad for a Christmas party being held in Milford. It's a writers group and I feel like you are supposed to attend."

The words were coming from a female who had befriended me years before at the church I had been attending, one which, although I am not a member, I have considered my "home" church in the northeast for several years. I took her "word from the Lord" into consideration.

"I'm already writing for magazines and still occasionally for the newspaper in Tennessee. I don't see why I need a writers group," I responded.

"Well, you don't have to go, but like I said, I felt led by the Lord to tell you to go."

"I'll think about it."

My "thinking" turned into obedience. The group was having what they called their "Jingle Mingle" for the holiday and had branched out by way of the newspaper-- seeking other writers to attend and possibly join their group. What I realized, however, was that the purpose the Lord had for my attending the holiday get-together was actually for me to meet members of another writers group who also showed up for the Christmas gathering. It was a group that met at Barnes and Noble on Thursday evenings. They extended an invitation to all of us to visit their meeting.

The Milford Writers Group welcomed all of us and invited us to read a sample of our work to those gathered, if we were so disposed. I looked at the group of four to my left-the members of the Barnes and Noble group. One woman in particular was quite brash; I laughed easily and heartily as she read a piece she had brought which was very funny. I instantly felt attracted to the members of their group, who seemed to share a similar sense of humor and a close bond. I told them that I intended on joining them at their next meeting.

I arrived at Barnes and Noble the following Thursday. I met several other writers who had not attended the Milford Group's holiday gathering, many of which had just recently decided to come back to the group after some lengthy absences.

Hearing that I was a Christian who wrote for a Christian magazine in Tennessee did not immediately ingratiate me to members of the group. In fact, the news rather worked against me. Most of the attendees claimed no religious affiliation; some were quite vocal about their dislike of Christianity and its followers, and at the very least, extremely suspect toward anyone claiming to be Christian. Each week, I read my most recent article for the magazine for the group to proof and critique. I loved hearing their comments and suggestions.

One of the most touching moments was the night I read aloud my article/essay on friendship. The "brash" woman was overcome with emotion as I shared some of the poignant stories, memories of the recent loss of her lifelong best friend had come crashing down like waves, hitting unexpectedly, deeply, emotionally. She was surprised by the tears, which were flowing down her cheeks and which she couldn't seem to control or reign in, tears she thought had been totally spent.

On another evening, I read my story titled, "Are You Paranoid or Are People Really Watching You?" wherein I addressed the subject of hypocrisy. It was the group's favorite. Unfortunately, they easily recognized and related their own numerous examples of witnessing people claiming Christ as their Savior but without demonstrating what should have been its matching behavior. It was very eye-opening. I love relating the story and the reaction of the members of the group whenever I get the chance. It has an impact on the Christians I tell, who often repent after realizing that they have been guilty of some of the same bad behaviors included in the article.

We became a very unusual group of unlikely friends. One friendship in particular stands out. One of the members in the group and I would be described as polar opposites and initially, had quite an adversarial relationship. Despite coming from differing angles on virtually every subject imaginable, we have become good friends. We began referring to ourselves as Oil and Water, and often carpool to the writer's group meetings, laughing most of the way there. Having found humor as a common ground, we have become valued friends.

THE PEN (AND PRAYER): MIGHTIER THAN THE SWORD

After I had been a member of the writers' group long enough for most of their overt skepticism of me to have subsided, I began asking if it would be okay with them if I were to send concerns they had to my church in Tennessee to have them prayed over. Every Wednesday evening church members gather for a service and prayer. Congregants pick up a list of prayer requests along with a stack of cards to sign as confirmation that they have prayed for each request personally. They are then mailed to recipients of the prayers.

Apparently, they didn't object. It soon became standard operating procedure for me to ask them about their concerns, and for them to respond. I emailed their requests to my church. The signed cards were mailed to me; I handed them out at the next meeting. The prayers offered by strangers were valued and worked! There were several healings which had taken place within the group itself or their family members.

There was always something presented for prayer. A friend or family member was battling cancer. Another member of the group desperately needed a job. There was trouble at home. Children were sick or rebelling. I prayed; my church prayed.

One member asked me to pray for her male friend. He had been diagnosed as having lung cancer. I turned the request into my church and I prayed for him. I had never met him, but a few weeks later, he showed up at the writers meeting. I announced to those gathered that I wanted our next meeting to be held at my house. It would be a Christmas party. I wondered if the new guy I had prayed for would bring his guitar and sing for us. I had been assured that he was very talented.

The night was perfect. Everyone showed up with holiday goodies and cheer. We laughed and shared stories. Some members read something they had written for the special gathering of what had now become close friends.

The crowd gradually thinned until there were only four of us left. I could feel the presence of God. I knew He had something in mind. I asked "guitar man" if he minded if I prayed for him. He placed the guitar down gently next to his chair. I took out my anointing oil, anointed his forehead and prayed for his healing. When I finished the prayer, another man said. "Can you pray for others as well?" I anointed and prayed for all of them that night. The "Glory Cloud" filled the room. I knew to expect miracles.

Those needing healing were healed. "Guitar man" not only uses his vast array of musical talents: singer, songwriter, musician--he is now a published author as well. One member who needed a job got one. She recently celebrated her sixth anniversary in the position which she enjoys and which also pays well.

One brisk night, one of my favorite members in the group took me aside after the meeting. I had thrown out the usual question, "Any prayer requests?" He requested prayer for his daughter. I began praying that night and also turned his request in to my church.

I returned to Tennessee. Months later, I received an email from him. He shared the impact the Lord having sent me to their group had made upon his life.

"You appeared in our tight little writing group as if out of nowhere. Your breezy humor and forthright personality injected a breath of uncommon air to our creativity. You claimed that God had spoken to you and told you to join us, guiding you all the way from Tennessee to New England. Our group however, was politely skeptical.

Often you would share with us the messages you received from God. In your lighthearted way-- you encouraged us to speak to God. "God listens to everyone," you reassured us. "Even about the smallest things," you said.

Later, a loved one in our immediate family contracted stage four cancer.

She fought it, and after radical surgery and invasive chemotherapy, she started to recover. By that time, we could see the beginning of depression edging in. But there was a further price to pay. She was fired from her job and try as she could, was unable to get another one. The depression deepened and I contacted you and asked you to use your connection with God and pray for our daughter, exercising your compassion. Gratefully, you did so. Soon after, we witnessed a change in our loved one. She gained back her animation and love of life.

Soon, her new happiness aided her into getting a job and resuming her old life as before. I will always be grateful to you for strengthening my own belief and using your own great faith and union with the Almighty."

PRISON GUY

So, I was happily writing the magazine stories and inviting the group to critique them when the Lord, through His "still, small voice" gave me a new directive.

"Write your memoir."

As usual, the fight of reasoning began.

"But Lord, I'm not famous! Only actors, politicians and the renowned are able to sell memoirs. No one is interested in reading about my life! The book wouldn't sell!"

"Write your memoir."

I titled it "The Question." I had to admit. It was pretty funny and actually interesting, since I have led quite an extraordinary life. One night, as we were all gathered at the book store, we noticed a young, handsome, dark-haired man reading a book about the mob. He was seated directly across from our table and apparently overheard our entire conversation, the last of which was me reading the latest excerpt from my memoir. It included my kidnapping, a break in, having been strangled by a total stranger, an experience with a Peeping Tom, and several near-death experiences.

Finally, the young man could contain his thoughts no more. He got up, approached our table and addressed me. His gestures, style and manner of speech reminded me of the stereotypical depiction of mobsters portrayed in the movie *The Godfather*.

"Lady, I've been around," he asserted. Nodding his head lightly to one side, he shrugged his shoulders and opened his hands in a gesture of explanation. "I've seen some things in my life. I know some people… if you catch what I'm saying. I've even, well…I've done some time. I was in prison. But I have NEVER in my life heard anything like what you have been reading!"

I smiled.

"Are those stories true?"

"They sure are! God has rescued me out of a lot of tough places!" We smiled at one another.

The evening ended and we all rose to leave, however, each week thereafter the same young man was seated in the same chair across from us. He was there to hear what was being read. He offered to buy me tea or coffee--often gave me a gift card for the café' within Barnes and Noble and was always sweet. Although he told us his name once, none of us could remember it, so we always referred to him as "Prison Guy."

One night, several weeks later, I, along with the petite schoolteacher who was part of the group, arrived early. She sat down; I remained standing as Prison Guy approached. I remember noticing that he didn't seem himself. He seemed somewhat off that night--like something was bothering him.

"How are you tonight?" I questioned.

"Not so good," was his lackluster response.

"Why? What's wrong?" I pressed.

"Well, I had a little run of bad luck over the week end. I lost $78 grand at the track in Jersey."

I knew this was serious. It was as though I had been enabled to see into the very depths of his being, the fear, the remorse, the anguish, which in the space of a week end had now taken over his life.

Whenever I describe this moment to others, I always jokingly say that Pamela--like Elvis--left the building. But I am very serious when I relate that it was indeed God's Holy Spirit who spoke through me to Prison Guy. What proceeded forth out of my mouth went straight into his inner man. It's the only way I know how to explain it.

I remember starting out with the comment, "You know, you do not have to live that lifestyle. God has something better for your life--if you will accept it." After saying that, the words absolutely poured forth. The schoolteacher's mouth gaped open, the Glory Cloud arrived once again, and all of us were glowing. I have no recollection of the words that came forth from me to him, but I do remember the profoundness of the moment and the effect it had on all three of us.

To this day, I have always wondered what became of Prison Guy. We never saw him again, and our meeting place eventually changed. I have asked the Lord several times to let me see him again. I want to know his fate. I have so many questions. What I do know are these assurances:

Isa 55:11: So shall my word be that goeth forth out of my mouth: it shall not return unto me void, but it shall accomplish that which I please, and it shall prosper in the thing whereto I sent it.

1Co 3:6: I have planted, Apollos watered; but God gave the increase.

JEREMIAH WAS NOT A BULLFROG

I attended a very ritual-oriented church when I was a child. After leaving my faith for years, I was "Born Again" on my bedroom floor in a duplex in Wichita Falls, Texas. It was extremely rare for me to attend a service in the denomination afterwards. I had chosen to attend other denominations instead, ones less ritual-based.

Once it became common knowledge that the denomination had departed from the tenets of the faith, I announced adamantly, "I will never set foot in that church again the rest of my life." As far as I am concerned, "Ichabod" is written on it. "Ichabod means "inglorious" or "there is no glory" (and I have often heard another definition: "The glory of the Lord has departed").

One Sunday afternoon, a friend of mine invited me to attend a free organ recital in West Haven, CT. It was to be held at a church on "The Green," the term used in New England for the Town Square. My first question to her was, "Which church?"

"I don't know, a Christian church, maybe a Congregational one."

"Can't you find out?" I asked, pressing.

"What difference does it make? It's in a church and it's free!"

"It matters to me because I've told you before that there are certain churches which have chosen to leave the doctrines of the faith and I refuse to set foot in them."

"I'm sure it's OK."

I still had my church attire on when she picked me up. My champagne colored high heels, leopard bag, and olive green silk suit was topped off with a "Fascinator," the tiny hat that protrudes from the side of one's head. My friend's husband often accused me of stealing my hats off an organ grinder's monkey.

I thought, 'What are the chances it will be that denomination?'

We pulled up and parked across the street from the church. Sure enough, it was the church I refused to attend.

"Oh, come on," she urged. "Don't be so rigid. It's not a service. It's just a recital."

"No."

"What will you do? Sit in the car for an hour?"

"There's a gazebo on the Green. I will go sit there for the duration."

"Are you sure?"

"Yes."

I walked past the gazebo and sat down on a bench instead. There was another bench to the left. Two teen-aged girls sat on it as a younger male friend chose to make rounds on his skateboard. They viewed my presence with wariness. I was a stranger on their turf. I must have looked very odd to them dressed in my Sunday best.

One of the girls was cursing and quite boisterous. The other was more reticent.

We all turned our attention to a group of people walking toward the church.

"OOOOOhhhweee! Helllllloooo there!" the boisterous one had apparently noticed a good looking teenager walking with the group.

"Don't go in there! Come over here!" she ordered, to no avail. She spoke fairly loudly, but not enough for him to hear---only loudly enough to embarrass her friend.

"Stop it! He will hear you!"

"I don't care. I hope he does! OOOOhhhweee! What's going on over there anyway?" She asked to no one in particular.

"There's an organ recital going on," I offered.

She turned her full attention toward me.

"What's an organ?"

At first I thought she was being facetious. Then I realized she really didn't know which was baffling to me.

"You know. It's similar to a piano…has keys… sounds emit from large pipes? An instrument Bach or Beethoven used…?" (Note to self: good Luck with those names being recognized, Pamela. The girl doesn't even know what an organ is-- much less composers from a time before last year).

The other girl nodded and helped explain.

"Oh, yeah."

"Well, if you like the guy so much, why don't you go over and attend?" I offered. "Maybe you can meet him. It's free."

"Yeah! Hey, let's go!" she said to her friend.

"I don't want to go over there!" The other girl whined and rebelled as the boisterous one grabbed her arm and tried unsuccessfully to pull her in the direction of the church.

Just then, a group of four male teenagers approached.

"Hey, you wanna go over to that church with me?" she yelled out to them.

"H--L No! Why in the world would I want to go to some (expletive) church? The last thing in the world I want to do on a Sunday is go to some (expletive) church!"

She danced around, ooohing and ahhhhing all the while, as she tried to explain about the cute boy.

The guys all glanced toward me and then began selecting their places in the gazebo and on its steps. The main guy was front and center. I knew I was being viewed with great curiosity and not a small amount of suspicion. I sensed the question rolling around in their minds. What was *I* doing sitting there... in my church lady clothes--in their domain? They glanced toward their female friends with raised eyebrows, curious as to a potential connection to me. Their unasked questions answered with disinterested shrugs.

'Well, Lord,' I thought. 'I'm here for a reason. I might as well go for it.'

Addressing the main guy's comments, I threw out a question.

"So, is the reason going to church is the last thing you would want to do on a Sunday about God or about something else?" I asked casually.

He looked at me, cocking his head sideways before answering.

"H--L No! It doesn't have anything to do with God! I don't believe in God!!! I'm tired. I worked all week end!"

"You don't believe in *GOD*? How do you explain the fact that you're *breathing*?" I responded.

"I'm breathing because my parents had sex!" he laughed, nodding to his friends who joined in with laughter and mumbled assents.

"*None* of you believe in God?"

"No!" They all shouted in unison, adamant in their unbelief.

A young black guy with a bright cherry red afro peeking out from under a ball cap shot a satanic symbol in my direction with his fingers.

"I believe in SATAN! I am a Satan worshiper!"

"SERIOUSLY?"

"Yeah."

Then an intense exchange began. I prodded, questioning their beliefs--or lack thereof. They took turns answering and posing questions about an allegedly "good" God who allows terrible things to happen. I presented the case for Christ, and some answers the Holy Spirit so beautifully gave in my time of need.

One of them argued in defense of Buddha. The black guy explained his decision to follow Satan. He made his way down the steps and slowly eased his way over nearer my bench.

"Let me ask you something," I said. "Why would you want to serve Satan rather than God?"

"Because he will give me fame and fortune!" he shouted, once again displaying the satanic symbol. "I will be RICH!"

"Haven't you read all the tragic stories of people who make it to the "top" in this world, and yet, find themselves with no true friends, no real friends and then die after having either committed suicide or having overdosed on drugs? They always seem to wonder or question whether their so-called "friends" are with them because they care about them-- or if they are after what their money, possessions and fame can get them. They never really know. See those guys at the gazebo? You never have to wonder about them. You have nothing to offer them but yourself. But that's what they want...you--just for who you really are. Not for what you have. Besides, everyone knows that in the end, Satan is the loser. God wins! Why would you want to serve the loser?"

He glanced down and shrugged.

Afterward, we talked softly. I asked him about his life. He revealed some very disturbing problems he was facing.

"You know, we are far enough away that your friends have no idea what we are saying. What I would like to do is pray for you...quietly, without anyone knowing. You can sit on the other end of this bench. We will keep our eyes open so they don't know what we're doing. Would that be ok?"

He eyed me suspiciously…as though I might hurt him or something.

"Look at me for goodness sakes! I'm church lady--in heels! What am I going to do to you?"

He smiled shyly and then sat down on the end of the bench.

I prayed for him with our eyes open, looking as though we were having a conversation. Afterwards he got up, glanced at me, said a quiet "thank you" and walked back over to the gazebo. He made his way up the steps, turned, looked at me and then gave the symbol of Satan.

I just smiled and kind of shook my head little bit.He had to keep up appearances in front of his friends. I understood. It's all about peer pressure and saving face at their age. I turned my attention to the leader of the group.

"So, why are you so against believing in God?"

"He's never done a thing for me!"

"Like I said, you're breathing aren't you?"

He came up with a litany of bad things that had happened in his life, disappointments, etc., none of which God was responsible for, which I attempted to explain.

The guy who was making a case for belief in Buddha piped in.

We spent quite a bit of time on that subject. The bottom line with him was that his dad had died. Once again, in his estimation, God was to blame.

The exchange between the four teenagers continued for a long time. I finally asked the leader of the group what his name was. I wasn't prepared for his answer.

"Jeremiah."

I could tell he instinctively knew what my reaction was going to be.

"Are you kidding? You're named after one of the Major Prophets in the Bible!"

"I knew you were gonna say that! But I'm not! I'm named after the bull frog song. Seriously, that's who my parents named me after."

"I don't believe it. I believe that is the name that the Lord wanted you to have. He has a cool future designed for you. Whether you believe it or not --it's the truth."

"Well, I don't believe it. He's never done anything for me."

I addressed all of them.

"Okay you guys. This is what I'm going to do. I'm going to pray for all of you--behind your backs." I smiled. "You can't stop me from praying for you! I love it! It's a power and ability that I have that you can't do anything about! I'm going to pray that God shows Himself to you in dreams and visions. And that you'll be very much aware that He exists. I know He will answer and I know he will help you."

Glancing over, I saw people exiting the church. I rose from the bench and walked over in front of them.

"I have to go, but I want to sing you a song before I leave.

"No, man!" they all grumbled and complained in unison with audible moans and groans at the thought of my singing to them.

"You'll live."

I opened my mouth and belted out *Amazing Grace*, black gospel style, with everything I had in me. It had been a long time since I had done such a thing. I wasn't expecting their reaction.

"Wow!!!" The professing Buddhist was the first to vocalize his reaction.

"Man!!! You should be on American Idol!!!" Jeremiah said.

The young black guy started singing some form of rap at the same time I was singing. They told him to shut up.

I laughed. I told them that it was God who brought me there to meet them that day, that it was no accident, that it was no coincidence.

"He wants to let you know that He really does exist…and that he loves you."

I saw my friend exiting the church, perfect timing. I smiled at my new-found motley assortment of unwilling, unlikely friends, and then walked away. We arrived at her car at the same time.

"I hope you weren't bored while I was at the recital."

I had been with the teenagers for over an hour.

"No, not at all." I smiled.

A few weeks later, some Christian friends of mine wanted to hold a going away party for me. It was quite touching. I never knew whether or not I would be returning. It was always up to the Lord. Consequently, each time I was leaving, my friends would have a going away party in my honor since we never knew if we would ever see one another again. Even on those rare occasions when we knew we would see each other again, we also knew it would probably be a long time before it happened.

The ultimate, "go-to" girl, party planner was my friend Stephney. This time, she suggested that my party be held at Chili's in Milford, Connecticut. It was not where I would've chosen, but she was the one in charge of planning it and arranging everything so I let her choose the location.

The party was somewhat last-minute, (I didn't always know when I would be called upon to leave), so only a handful of us showed up that day at lunch.

I had chosen to wear a new suit which none of the girls had seen. They admired the suit and my recently acquired pair of high heels. Fashion was almost always a topic of conversation, especially between Stephney and me. They also wanted to know the details about this trip, who God had sent me to, what He had been speaking to me, how I had been used by Him.

I had barely begun to answer their questions when I caught sight of a figure in my peripheral vision. Although I did not see the person's face--whoever it was had on a hoodie and was moving quickly toward the exit. There was something familiar about the person's presence--despite the anonymity afforded by his/her garb. I stood up, abruptly told my friends I would be right back, and raced around the table and toward the door. By the time I got outside, the person had made it halfway across the parking lot.Realizing that I didn't have much time, I took a chance and screamed out.

"Jeremiah!" I screamed, trusting my instincts.

Stopping in his tracks, the person in the hoodie whirled around and faced me. Sure enough--it was him!

"It's *ME*! Church Lady! Is this *GOD* or what?" I smiled, arms opened wide.

He shook his head in disbelief. We were in a totally different town several weeks after we had met that day on the green.

"Ah, Man! I can't believe this!"

"Why? I told you God was after you," I laughed.

"Man, it's just that this is, like, one of the worst days of my entire life!"

"Why? What happened?"

"I got accused of doing something in school that I didn't do--so I got suspended, my girlfriend broke up with me and my truck broke down. I have to walk all the way back home."

"I can give you a ride. I'll take you home."

"Nah, I'll walk. I'll be OK."

"But it's two towns away! Twenty or thirty miles!"

"I'll be all right."

"Listen. You know this is the Lord. What are the chances we would see each other again, at this moment, miles away from where we met-- in a different town altogether? God arranged for me to be here today for *you*. He wants you to know that he is actively pursuing you with his love. He has seen everything that happened and He is on the scene to rescue. Surely you believe it now!"

He glanced down, shuffled his feet, and looked at me. A shy smile crept onto his face. I walked closer to him. Despite my high heels, he was a lot taller than me.

"Jeremiah, would you mind if I prayed for you? I would like to put my hand on your arm and say a prayer for you. Would that be OK?"

"Nah, I don't mind. You can."

I placed my hand on his arm and prayed right there in the middle of the parking lot. I felt the Lord's presence profoundly, and so did he. I could tell.

"Jeremiah, I barely know you-- but I love you. Jesus knows everything about you and He loves you more than I could possibly ever love you. I am so glad He allowed me to see you again, and used me to let you know that He is real. He has seen everything that has happened to you, and wants you to know that you are loved. Remember how I told you I was going to pray for you? Well, He has answered in a marvelous way! May I give you a hug? I will probably never see you again."

I gave him a big hug. I wasn't prepared for his response.

"Man! You just made my day!" He shook his head and tilted his face toward me. His eyes were sparkling, which made my heart melt. I loved this young man.

"Can't I give you a ride home? Please? I don't mind."

"Nah. I'm going to walk. I'll be fine now." He smiled and walked away.

I walked back inside.

"I'm ready to tell you the story about my trip, and Stephney, you are a part of it. It truly was the Lord who told you to hold my party here today."

Although I returned to Connecticut several times after that trip, I never ran into Jeremiah again. He is in Jesus' hands, where I am certain he is being carefully safeguarded, loved and watched over.

FROM OUR TOWN TO NEWTOWN

I remember hearing the news as it was unfolding. As was the case with the rest of the nation, I was shocked, grief-stricken, horrified. I couldn't believe what I was hearing. A young man had entered Sandy Hook Elementary School in Newtown, Connecticut and began shooting. The shooter was finally fatally wounded, but only after he had extinguished the lives of 26 people; 20 of which were young children.

Two months prior to the shooting, I had left Connecticut and headed back to my other residence in Tennessee. I had been sent to Connecticut numerous times since the Lord called me there as an evangelist in the fall of 2000. Newtown is located 23 miles from the town where I had been staying for the past 13 years.

The Sunday morning after the tragedy, people were assembled in churches all over the nation. I would venture to say that there probably wasn't one minister who failed to call for prayer for the families of the victims. My church was no exception. Our Pastor began the morning service with a call for God to send the kind of comfort only He can give, His Holy Spirit.

The congregation bowed their heads and besought God on behalf of the suffering strangers. Nothing short of God Almighty could heal that kind of pain. I knew from experience. I winced at the thought of the long grief-process which awaited the family members. When tragedy hits, the right words often fail us. Sometimes all we can say is, "Lord Jesus, help them." It's not the eloquence of the prayer that moves the heart of God; it's the heart of compassion with which it is presented.

I had thought my evangelism trips to Connecticut were over when I left in the fall of 2012, but the Lord surprised me by calling me there once again in September/2013. I stayed with a friend who lives a block from the waters of Long Island Sound. The weather was unseasonably warm and wonderful.

I watched with interest as state workers were cutting limbs from trees which were obstructing power lines. The workers moved up the roads gradually over a span of a few weeks, finally landing at the house directly across the street from where I was staying. I had gone shopping the day before and had left the items in my car. The following day, as I retrieved the items from my car, a man in a hardhat walked over and approached me.

"Are you the one from Tennessee?" (He saw my license plate).

"Yes I am," I said with a smile.

"Boy, are you lucky! My parents moved down around Chattanooga and when I retire I'm moving there!"

It wasn't long after that he told me there were, "just too many memories to stay any longer in Connecticut."

The man in the hardhat, the man who ventured across the street to speak to me was the father of one of the victims shot to death in Newtown. My heart instantly went out to him. Tears welled up as he shared what he knew of his daughter's final moments.

We talked about their close relationship and what a blessing she had been to him. We both began to tear up. I told him that I, too, had lost a daughter many years before.

"It's very hard."

As I stood there with him that day, I couldn't help but remember ten months before, as we prayed for the victims' families at my church. We prayed for God to send people to minister to them. I felt honored and privileged to be among those He sent.

HEAL THE SICK

Matt 10:8 Heal the sick, cleanse the lepers, raise the dead, cast out devils: freely ye have received, freely give.

Luke 9:2: And he sent them to preach the kingdom of God, and to heal the sick.

Luke 10:9: And heal the sick that are therein, and say unto them, The kingdom of God is come nigh unto you.

Jim had called a friend of mine and asked her to have me get in touch with him. He said it was important. Although we had not seen each other in a long time, whenever Jim met someone who was sick, he automatically thought of me. Having witnessed the Lord sending me to anoint and pray for the sick over a period of several years, (including his mother), and seeing miraculous healings occur as a result had made a tremendous impact on Jim's faith in God's ability to heal.

"What's up?"

"Thanks for getting back to me. The reason I asked you to call is that I know two people who need prayer. Both have stage four cancers. One works at a convenience store and is from another country. He's Muslim. I feel really bad for the guy because he's young and they don't give him any hope. I told him about you and that you pray for people and that I've seen people get healed. I told him I would have you stop by and pray for him. Will you do it?"

"He's Muslim?"

"Yes."

"You told him I'm a Christian?"

"Yes."

"And he doesn't mind if I pray for him in the name of Jesus?"

"No."

"So I'm supposed to pray for him in the convenience store?"

"Yes. I will go with you."

"Who is the other person?"

Jim explained that when he went to the doctor there was a male clerk at the hospital whom he had befriended. The man had been diagnosed with stage four cancer and initially, had gone through treatments. Nothing had worked. The outlook was bleak. Jim shared that I prayed for people and told him some of the miracles he had witnessed. He told him he would have me stop by the hospital and pray for him.

"We can go together."

"When?"

"Well, I will find out his schedule. He is off right now."

"OK."

Jim explained where his Muslin friend worked. I knew the location well. I also knew how to get to the hospital where the other man worked.

When I am in Connecticut, I attend a women's Bible study on Thursday mornings. Although it is held in a Baptist church, women from other denominations attend also. The group has morphed several times over the years; some women come and go, some have remained faithful for many years. I love attending. I have grown very close to several of the women. The exchanges between us often get quite animated; we learn a lot from one another. It is very uplifting to meet with other Christians to study the Word, give feedback and share experiences.

I was headed to the Bible study about a month after Jim had requested that I pray for his friend at the store. Jim was a procrastinator, so we had never gotten together to visit the young man. Since I knew Jim had paved the way by telling the guy about me, I figured I would just stop in by myself and pray. I knew time was of the essence, and enough of it had been wasted already.

I walked into the store. There was only one customer in the small retail area. I perceived that the customer was a frequent visitor and that I had probably interrupted a friendly exchange. The customer had a cup of coffee in one hand and an unlit cigarette in the other. I wasn't sure how I should approach the man behind the counter, so I just blurted it out and waited for a reaction.

'Hi!" I smiled. "I'm Jim's friend from Tennessee. I believe he told you about me? I pray for people?"

The lone customer was standing behind me. He cleared his throat. I turned around and faced him.

"Should I leave, go outside?" he asked.

I glanced back at the man behind the counter. He shrugged--indicating that didn't matter to him, if it didn't matter to me.

"No. You can stay. I'm just going to be a minute. I'm going to pray and then get on my way."

I turned my attention back to the young man. He smiled shyly.

"If you don't mind, may I touch your arm across the counter? The Bible says that we shall lay hands on the sick and they shall recover."

"Do you want to come around?" He asked.

"No, I can pray just as easily across the counter." I smiled.

The customer was still behind me and to the side. I could see him in my peripheral vision. I doubt that he was expecting what occurred next. As soon as I placed my hand on the young man's arm, the Glory of God filled the store. I could see that the young man was lit up--glowing, and I suspected that I was as well. I'm sure that the customer, an unwitting participant that morning, was a recipient of the incredible overwhelming presence of God as well.

I prayed for the healing power of God to manifest in his body, for him to live and not die and declare the glory of God. I commanded that cancer flee his body and there to be no ill effects from the disease that had previously ravaged his young life. The prayer stood out to me as being one of the most succinct I ever remember praying, short, sweet and to the point, yet delivered with love and faith.

He smiled profusely, still glowing. He kept thanking me again and again; as he offered me anything in the store I might want.

"Coffee? Something to eat? Anything, anything at all you would like?"

I appreciated his offer but declined.

Around a week later, I got in touch with Jim. I asked if he had seen his convenience store buddy.

"No. Why?"

"Well, I didn't want to wait any longer since I never know when I will be leaving so I went ahead and stopped at the store and prayed for him."

"You went there?"

"Yes."

"How did it go?"

"At first, I don't think he realized who I was, but he finally remembered you telling him about me and that I would pray for him."

"Jim, I would like to pray for the other man, the one at the hospital. Can you get me his cell phone number? I can pray for him over the phone if necessary. That works too if you recall."

He agreed to get the number.

I called the clerk and explained who I was. He said I could call him at exactly 4:30 p.m. That was when he would be in his car and could sit in the parking lot while I prayed. I called at exactly 4:30.

"Oh, I started to drive out of the parking lot. Just let me pull over." He was apologetic for the memory lapse.

His name was Carl.

"Carl, I was told that you have been diagnosed as having stage four cancer."
"Yes. I went through some treatments, but they made me so sick; I stopped quite a while back. Nothing was working anyway. I'm not going through that again."

"Well, Jesus is the healer. He works miracles. I've seen many, including several people who had cancer."

"I believe it."

"Well, I'm going to pray then."

"Ok."

I repeated much the same prayer as I had for the other young man. He thanked me for the prayer. I could feel that same powerful anointing of God despite the fact that the prayer had taken place over the phone.

Around a month after I had returned to Tennessee, I called Jim about a business matter; a friend needed his help. He offered his advice. We talked for several minutes before I remembered something very important, yet I delivered my question almost as an afterthought.

"Hey, did you ever hear anything about the two guys you asked me to pray for? Do you know what has become of them?"

"I didn't tell you?"

"No, Jim." I said, exasperated at his seemingly continual lack of recall. "We haven't spoken since then-- remember?"

"They're both healed! They told me to tell you and to thank you!"

I cried. I rarely cry out of sadness, but I almost always do when there is great joy.

HERE COMES THE RIGHTEOUS JUDGE

Remember the big barn in Bethany, CT, where the guy referred to me as a white blood cell? Once again, I was there for an evening of musical delight. I had barely entered the main room when I was approached by a man named Bill.*

"Have you been here before?"

"Yes, many times."

"I haven't seen you before."

"Well, I'm not always here. My home is in Tennessee."

"Really? What do you do?"

"I'm an evangelist."

I'm pretty sure my occupation was the last thing Bill was expecting to hear. But he was very engaged as he asked questions about the topic of evangelism. We continued our somewhat animated conversation. He said he was an attorney. That night, whether attempting to get a rise out of me-- or simply telling the truth, I couldn't be sure; he said he was an atheist.

We caught sight of one another in various rooms throughout the evening. I remember glancing over and seeing him sitting in a chair in the corner as I was docey do-ing, circling around joyfully with the crowd in the

Contra-dancing (similar to square dancing) room upstairs. He gave a smile and a wave. I still had my white faux fur coat on.

Later, both of us were now back downstairs.

"Hello again."

I told him I never meet anyone by accident that the Lord sends me to people. He wondered if I felt the Lord had sent me to him.

"I'm sure of it!" I responded with a smile.

I ran into him again the next month, then again on a subsequent evening. At one point, I gave him a copy of my book. He thanked me. The next two times I saw him, I asked if he had read my book. The answer was still the same.

"No."

I was very disappointed. I don't like waste, and to me it had been a waste of one of my books. I've been told that people rarely appreciate anything they don't pay for--that having "skin in the game" makes the difference. I was afraid that was the case.

I traveled back to Tennessee and then returned four months later.

Once again, there we were-- in front of each other. We both smiled. I asked the now familiar question, his answer remained the same. I finally gave up on him reading the book and indicated that he should give it to someone who he thought might actually read it. He suggested that he could return it and I could give it to someone else. I told him that would be fine.

Each time we met we talked briefly. I liked him, He had a good sense of humor and there was something sweet and appealing about his personality.

I stayed a couple months, and then headed back home.

Four months later I was back.

"I read your book!" He looked somewhat different. I perceived a subtle lightening of weights/ burdens in his life.

"Really?" I was elated! But when I asked his opinion about some of the stories specifically…he couldn't remember them. I began to doubt that he had actually read it. I believe he had read *some* of it.

The next time we met he looked completely different.

"Hey! I went to church!"

He explained that first he had gone to a denomination he had attended in the distant past. He didn't feel right in that church, so he found his way to a Pentecostal, fired-up black church where he was the only white man in the crowd.

"They believe in glossolalia!"(The proper term for the Biblical phenomenon known as speaking in tongues, it is found in 1 Corinthians chapter 12 and chapter 14). They laid hands on me and prayed! They really showed me love and embraced me as a fellow brother."

I was blown away with the news! How great that was. First of all, he had discernment. The first church he attended didn't "feel right," and there is a good reason why it didn't. That church has departed from the faith. *He* may not have known exactly *why* he didn't like it --but I did. I didn't say anything about my thoughts concerning it however…

Fast forward a couple months. It was Bethany night again and it was also just before I was scheduled to leave CT. I told the Lord I didn't want to go. His response was to show me a vision of the attorney's face. I knew He wanted me to see him again before I left. I had been there for around 30 minutes when I spotted him. Wow! His face was literally glowing. He was a changed man. It seemed as though every burden he had ever been under had been lifted.

"Hello there!"

"What a difference!" My surprise at the change in his appearance had tumbled out. "Something has definitely happened to you!"

"You think so? You can tell?"

"Absolutely! Your burdens have been lifted! I can see the difference."

"You're very intuitive." He smiled broadly. I chuckled at his use of that term. What he credited as intuition is somewhat similar to one of the definitions of the "gift of discernment" in 1 Corinthians chapter 12.

I told him that I was only there that night because of him. I said I fought God about attending that night and that was when I had been shown a vision of his face.

"Really?" he was seemingly delighted by the thought that the Lord wanted me to see him before I left.

"Really!"

I left a few days later. I was headed back to Tennessee and looking forward to some rest, which never happened.

I had been home approximately two months when the Lord told me to call Bill. He reminded me that not only did I have Bill's business card, but that I had stored it in a spot which was easy to find. I had not entered his information into my cell phone because I had never planned on calling Bill.

"Hello?"

"Is this the attorney, Bill?"

"Uh, yes." He didn't recognize my voice-- as was expected.

"Well are you busy?" Since I still had not identified myself, I knew he was hesitant to answer that question, possibly fearing that if he answered in the affirmative, he would be stuck in a conversation in which he would rather not be engaged.

"This is Pamela--the evangelist from Tennessee!" I had broken his reservations about the call.

"Oh!" I should have recognized your voice."

"Well, I has happily minding my own business when out of the blue, the Lord told me to call you. I figured something must be going on in your life. He also reminded me that you had given me your business card months ago, and thankfully, I had stashed it in an easy place to find."

Bill described what happened in his life the day *before*, and the day *of* my call.

"As you know, my youngest child, my daughter, is 24 years old. She lives in San Francisco. She has not spoken to me for the past six years, since she left home after high school. There are many reasons for this, but a lot has to do with my estrangement and divorce from her mother. This has been painful for me, and I suspect for her as well.

Just before Christmas this year, I got a long, detailed and well-thought-out letter from her. She reviewed her grievances against me and said that she was at a crossroad: should she continue to keep me out of her life, or risk letting me back in? Am I worth the trouble? Will she be hurt again by me?

As you can imagine, I was thrilled to get the letter, and of course troubled by her expression of anger towards me. The very next day, I got a call from you, Pamela, inquiring how I was doing. We hadn't seen each other since you were back in Connecticut.

I got the call from you as I was thinking how best to respond to my daughters letter. You told me God had sent you to me in my hour of need. Of course, I knew you were right.

As we talked, it became apparent that I needed to include in my response a reference to the love passage from I Corinthians13. Right there on the phone, with tears in my eyes, you prayed with me, asking the Lord to guide me in writing my response and reminding me that the Lord can do anything in our lives, even move mountains of pain, which block relationships with loved ones in our lives. It was clear to me that you were absolutely right. God had sent you to me at that moment, just when I needed His help.

When I composed my reply a few days later, I included this reference to the love verses in I Corinthians 13 at the end of my letter:

As a great poet once wrote:

Love is patient and kind; love is not jealous or boastful; it is not arrogant or rude. Love does not insist on its own way; it is not irritable or resentful; it does not rejoice at wrong, but rejoices in the right. Love bears all things, believes all things, hopes all things, endures all things. Love never ends.

That is how I want to love you and your brothers.

I know you have a decision to make. It is a crossroad in your life. Do you open yourself to having a father-daughter relationship with me, with all the risk that entails, or close yourself off from me again? I hope you're able to trust that I won't hurt you again. I want to live up to that trust, should you decide, as I hope you will, to give me another chance.

Love, Dad.

I haven't yet heard back from her. She is a brilliant young lady and I'm sure she's thinking carefully how to respond. As the love verses tell us, Love never ends. I wait patiently for her response."

This time, I found myself praying that I had been used as both red and white blood cells, bringing life and healing to this father and his daughter.

JIM

Ah Yes. Jim. He was ultimately one of the greatest success stories from the harvest field. In his defense, he had suffered mightily as a child at the hands of his abusive father--for seventeen long years. It had taken a huge toll on his life for many years. I told him numerous times that the only way to stop the ill effects would be for him to forgive his dad.

"He's dead!"

"It doesn't matter. Forgiveness helps you-- not him. You can do it, even if he's dead. Please do it for your sake. Just go ahead and forgive him. You can name everything you can think of that he did, or just do a general, 'I forgive everything,' but either way, just do it."

It would be years before he would heed that advice. Finally, he chose to forgive.

"It was like heat went all through my body. Everything changed. I could talk about him and no longer feel bad anymore. The bad feelings just left," he said.

Jim found Jesus, he found forgiveness, and he found peace.

"If I died today, I would feel good about it," he shared one day. "I have peace in my life."

Is Jim perfect? No. Did he quit his abundant use of expletives? No. He's a lot better about it though. He's more aware of how his choices affect others and himself. God will be working on him until he meets him face to face, as is the case with all of us. It's a lifelong process--this transformation stuff. The Lord working wonders in us from the inside out; out with the old, in with the new.

Throughout the years, I've told many people that there is only one thing wrong with the church. There are people in it! That statement has never failed to bring a smile. Everyone is in a different stage of growth. Some are brand new babes, some are very mature and others are somewhere in between. Cut people some slack. You may no longer have that bad behavior you are witnessing in someone else, but you used to.

Many times, I have heard people say in hushed tones, "Well, the church split over the color of carpet and drapes!" My response always remains the same. "Thank goodness it wasn't over something trivial!"

One of the greatest life lessons I have learned is to always have the right outfit handy. My top preference is to clothe myself with a good sense of humor; it is fashionable for every occasion.

Proverbs 17:22 A merry heart doeth good like a medicine: but a broken spirit drieth the bones.

"WRITE!"

Several years ago, I had a dream about an institution of higher learning. The name of the school was Boston University School of Theology. Sadly, I was ignorant of its existence. In the dream, I saw a school annual of sorts; I glanced through photos of all the faculty members. I barely recall the details of the dream now, but I awakened with the strong impression that I should call the university.

It felt awkward to call. I didn't really know what I should say. The administrative assistant answered. I told her that it probably sounded odd to hear from a stranger several states away who had dreamed about their university, one that I had never heard of before, but there must have been some reason why it had been shown to me.

I rehearsed the details of the dream, adding the part about seeing a type of year book with photographs of their faculty members. The administrative assistant asked if I had thought about attending their school. I reiterated my ignorance of its very existence until I had the dream. The school offered classes for Master's and Doctoral degrees. I admitted I had never finished my undergraduate degree. (Life interrupted, a small child, a divorce. My priorities shifted from education to our next meal).

Seemingly not hearing my confession, she went on to explain they were holding an essay contest addressing the subject of evangelism; the winner would receive a $25,000 scholarship. Did I want to enter? Once again, I explained that I was ineligible. I had not earned my undergraduate degree. Life had gotten in the way.

She asked if I wanted her to send me some information on the university. (I was *NEVER* going to attend their university!).I didn't know why the Lord had given me the dream, what His purpose might be, but, oh well, I figured it couldn't hurt to read a brochure about the university.

Several days later a package arrived.Included in the information the administrative assistant sent was a paper explaining the details of the $25,000 essay contest and how it should be submitted! I rolled my eyes.

"Lord, I explained to her **three times** that I'm *INELLIGIBLE!*"

"Write the essay," He said.

The paper explained that while several mainline denominations had been seeing a rapidly dwindling membership, some newer non-denominational churches were experiencing a rapid rise in congregants. They wanted an essay addressing potential reasons for the shift and answers as to how to increase the rolls in the churches which were experiencing decline.

"What in the world would I *say,* Lord? I don't know anything about the subject and remember that trivial detail? I'm *INELLIGIBLE!*"

"Sit down and start writing. I will give you what to say."

So I did. What was truly incredible was the response the essay received. First, I mailed a copy to the University. I explained its background and that I had been compelled to write it. I also admitted that I was ineligible for the award and therefore I was sending a copy as a gift to them.

I figured it would be pitched in "file 13." Four days later, I received a letter from the Dean of Admissions thanking me for it. He said it, "truly was a gift." I was floored by the letter. From there, the Lord took the essay into both local and far reaching places. I was instructed to stand and read it in several pulpits. It took exactly 17 minutes to read it aloud, after which, revival broke out in every church where it had been read.

I also read it to almost every person I encountered. This went on for a few years. I prayed that one day it could be published so more people could read it. That desire was fulfilled when Dean Hutson, Publisher/Editor of *Our Journey,* (a Christian magazine), agreed to publish it. As I read it to various people, I watched as their lives began to change. One man had committed a murder years before. It sparked a transformation that resulted in his eventual salvation. It is central to understanding what true evangelism is and our role in it. Here it is....

EVANGELISM IN THE 21ST CENTURY: How Can We Do It?

I will never forget that day. At three o'clock in the morning on Christmas Eve Day, the Lord awakened me out of a deep sleep and said, "You are going to be an evangelist." I responded with unequaled brilliance, "Huh? Could you repeat that, Lord?"

Wow! I was being called by God to evangelism! Visions crowded my mind.Thousands of people--pushing, shoving, attempting to get nearer to the pulpit, so they could hang on my every word, as if listening to me would be the same as listening to E.F. Hutton, because, as the old commercial claimed, "When E.F. Hutton speaks, **everyone** listens."

Not many days later, I was being led by God to knock on the doors of shacks.Poverty-stricken people with deeply-lined faces answered. God truly had called me to evangelism, but not the inflated ego-based visions that I had conjured, but His vision--meet people where they are, and meet them in a way they will never forget; meet them with unconditional love and compassion.

I have thought of the wide-ranging means and methods used throughout the years by members of the Body of Christ in various denominations. People with committees, programs, plans, all designed to draw people to Christ or to church. Those that are working have tapped into the most valuable resource available, and without which, no man can succeed. This resource is God Almighty.

His Word states, *"Except The Lord build the house, they labour in vain that build it"* and *"if any of you lack wisdom, let him ask of God, that giveth to all men liberally, and upbraideth not, and it shall be given him."* So, first you must be aware that if anything is to be accomplished in the area of evangelism, it must be God who is building the house, and his house encompasses the entire Body of Christ, no matter what flavor. Be sure to check your motives. Is your motive to build *"your"* church? Or is it to build *"The"* church?

Second, you are at His mercy for true wisdom; that wisdom which comes from God alone… *"For who hath known the mind of The Lord? Or who hath been his Counselor?" "Because the foolishness of God is wiser than men; and the weakness of God is stronger than men…But God hath chosen the foolish things of the world to confound the wise, and God hath chosen the weak things of the world to confound the things which are mighty. And base things of the world, and things which are despised, hath God chosen, yea, and things which are not, to bring to naught things that are…* (Why?) *…That no flesh should glory in His presence. For who hath known the mind of The Lord, that he may instruct Him? But, we have the mind of Christ."*

So, here we have it – an incredible key to the furtherance of the gospel in every way. We may tap into the very mind of Christ. That glorious, majestic, unfathomable, omniscient mind that He makes very clear is so much

169

higher than our finite, carnal mind.He not only allows us access into His divine resource of information, which is so vast we could never comprehend the heights nor the depths of it, but along with it, He gives us the promise that the word which goes forth out of His mouth *shall* not return unto Him void, but it *shall* accomplish that which He pleases, and it *shall* prosper where He sends it.

He has established then that *He* must build the work and *He* must provide the wisdom. This requires us to let *Him* be in control and it also requires that we have such a relationship with Him that we can hear His voice. It has already been established in the scriptures written above, that if we need wisdom, we may receive it *liberally,* from Him, if we know His voice. Jesus states that we hear His voice, He calls us by name, leads us out, puts us forth, goes before us, we follow Him and know His voice. We will not follow a stranger, but will run from him, because we do not know the voice of strangers.

The way we ask and receive is through prayer. Peter asserts that we were left an example, Jesus Christ, that we should follow his steps.Well, what were His steps? His first call to us was to *"repent;"* His second was for us to follow Him. After His command to, *"Follow me,"* He gave a promise, *"and I will make you fishers of men."* This having been said to fishermen named Peter and Andrew.

How can we do it? Follow Him. His first act was to call in some help. Some buddies, to help with the task at hand; regular folks, who would leave *everything* to follow Him-- including their families. He then taught, preached and healed. He had quite the following since He was performing great miracles, and yet, did he not say that, *"Greater works than these shall ye do?"*

When Jesus addressed the disciples in the Sermon on the Mount, He gave them specific instructions as to how to behave properly. This type of behavior was in total contrast to the "world's" behavior, and was so radical that the people were literally *"astonished at His doctrine."* Why were the people astonished? Every mandate for their behavior was an affront to the flesh. He wanted them to drop "self" at their God and surrender to the only true and living God, who offered life, and life more abundantly to those who would believe.

Jesus was not trying to draw attention to Himself, but conversely, He healed and performed miracles, often with the command that they *"tell no man."* The flesh screams for accolades, the Spirit does things in secret, and delights in anonymity. God receives all the glory, and the man is rewarded openly by the Lord.

Jesus' next task was to show His disciples who they were to minister to, and to try to explain what He was doing to the religious leaders of the day. The "publicans" (tax collectors) and sinners came and sat down with Him. They were drawn to Him. Why were sinners drawn to Him? He was love. Why were the Pharisees so repulsed by Him? He was love. He was inward, they were outward. *"For the Lord seeth not as man seeth; for man looketh on the outward appearance, but the Lord looketh on the heart."*

I cannot begin to share all the many times that God has directed me to go and minister to a person that was so repulsive on the outside, that it was difficult to make my flesh obey the Spirit of God. These instances are termed "friendship evangelism." God leads you to a person, tells you what to do, and what to say, you obey the call, and watch God work.

For example, during one season of His call on my life, He led me to old, dirty, stinking men who wore ragged clothes and had tobacco spittle running down their faces.They were all full-fledged alcoholics, and many were bound by horrible sins that I will not share.

One man in particular lived in a tiny camper with no electricity. I would visit and talk with him whenever the Lord impressed me. We developed a friendship. After quite some time had elapsed, I was prompted to invite him to church, and after meeting all his objections, he agreed. This man had not been in a church in over fifty years. I arrived to pick him up and he was drunk. He said if I would take him in that condition, he would still go. So I helped him into my car.

When we arrived, the effects of the alcohol had increased, so I asked some men of the church to help me get him inside. We had to *carry* him in. I was so thankful that this church happened to be a non-denominational church that would allow anybody in any condition, in their church service. Their special outreach was to those who were totally bound by alcohol, drugs, and sin of all kinds; those desperately in need of deliverance.

We sat my friend down on a chair in the back of the church. The preacher began his sermon. Unfortunately, my inebriated friend also had a hearing problem, and whenever he made a comment, it was out there for the entire congregation to hear. He looked at me and yelled, "Why that preacher, he's a really preachin' it, ain't he? Why that preacher, he's a preachin' the truth!"

When the pastor realized that my friend's behavior was not going to get any better, he asked all the members to get up from their seats, gather around the man in the back, lay hands on him, and pray earnestly for him. This lasted for several minutes. My friend bowed his head, humbly received their loving prayers, and the service ended. I drove him home in relative quiet and bid him goodbye.

I did not see him for several weeks after that, and when I did, he seemed somewhat changed. We talked and laughed, and I went on my way. About two months later, I went to visit someone in the nursing home, and as I was going in, I was met by a man on the way out who called my name. I did not know the man--until he introduced himself. It was my friend. He was clean, his hair was neatly combed, and his face literally glowed. He had on nice clothes, and told me he had quit drinking and chewing tobacco, and had moved into proper housing. His entire life had changed; he had met Jesus Christ. *"Love covers a multitude of sins."* And the angels in heaven were rejoicing. This is evangelism in the 21st century. The love of God poured out to others by His people. The methods will differ, but the heart will be the same.

173

It has already been noticed that God has been increasing the flock in some churches which have proven that they are willing to allow the Holy Spirit to reign in their lives and in their church. The same openness to God's will and Spirit that John Wesley and other Christians of old understood firsthand. He asserted that, "The church itself must be flexible enough in its orders and processes to follow wherever the Spirit seems to lead. Every true church must be constantly making adjustments to new challenges and new situations, keeping always the solid, sure, scriptural basis of the Christian life."

A friend of mine recently shared a story that she had heard of a service which had taken place in New Jersey. A local pastor had shared his testimony in regard to evangelism. While praying one day, The Lord directed him to place an ad in the local paper, offering prayer to anyone in need, for any reason, and that they should hold the event at the local park in town. Hundreds came, most were un-churched. They were hungry for love and prayer. Jesus' command was that we "*go out to the highways and byways and compel people to come in.*" His design was for Christians to be nourished and equipped for the work of the ministry at their local church, and if that was being accomplished, the flock would fulfill its call to make disciples.

The harvest is white; the laborers are few. There is a key problem-the lack of the fear of God. Many church members fear man, and until your fear of God is greater than your fear of man, effective witnessing will not take place. An obvious example would be David and Goliath. David feared God and did not look at the circumstances.

Often in my years as a Christian, the Spirit of God has told me to approach someone who, according to their outward appearance, I would never have approached. Big, burly men with tattoos and chains hanging from their belts, and who had Intimidating looks on their faces, as I spoke to them by The Spirit of God, I would see their faces change. Their deep vulnerability would show through as I shared God's love for them. Many times throughout the Word of God, He admonished His people, *"Be not afraid of their faces."* He wanted us to go beyond the outer man to the hidden man of the heart.

Years ago, I was kidnapped and robbed at knife and gunpoint and was held for twelve hours. I was a relatively new Christian at the time and did not have a vast knowledge of the Bible. I did know Psalm 91 and it gave me the faith and strength to make it through. I knew God's promises were true and I held fast to that fact. Even though the circumstances were bad, The Lord still enabled me to witness my faith to them.

One thing that held them in amazement was my lack of fear. I did not scream when the gun was shoved against my temple by one man, nor when the knife was pressed against my side by the other. The fear of God, rather than man, enabled me to react (or not react) in such a way that it captured their interest and opened the door to my witnessing to them. I believed my God was able to deliver me from the snare of the fowler --and it was so.

There was a church split over the introduction of a new contemporary form of praise and worship. It happened over *200* years ago-the pastor was John Bunyun and the offense was the introduction of hymns. There is great reason to be concerned about mainline denominations today. They are losing people by the droves. Why? They are unwilling to "make adjustments to new challenges and new situations."

Do they really think that a style of service that has had very little change in over 200 years will attract the youth of today? If they do, they need to wake up before the doors are closed on their church. That is one of the major problems--it has become "their" church rather than "God's" church. If people would crucify their flesh and be open to the Spirit of God-- things would change. If they would agree to "get out of the way" then God could move.

How can we do it? One Methodist minister shared a wonderful testimony of The Lords' transformation of his church. He went before the Lord and said, "Lord, if there is anyone who is a hindrance to your work in our congregation, I promise I will not hold back, I will have the boldness to tell them so we can go forth! Just reveal to me who it is." The Lord responded immediately, "It's YOU!"

He repented and promised to get out of the way and let the Spirit of God rule and reign in his church. The number of members has grown from just over 100 to over 500; the music used is contemporary praise and worship, and there are healing teams who anoint people with oil at the end of each service--an average of 150 people go forward for prayer each Sunday. Wow! What fantastic results are achieved when the Lord is in control! All He requests is that we, *"Be not afraid, only believe."*

I would encourage all pastors to have a core group of people to pray at the church for a Spirit of revival, repentance, and renewal to visit their pastor and congregation, and that they would be able to "hear what the Spirit of God is saying to the church," theirs in particular. I would also encourage them to pray for the Spirit of God to have control in their lives and in their church, and that the gifts and fruit of the Spirit would continually be manifest in the lives of each member.

I began with the principle that except the Lord build the house--they labor in vain who build it. No denomination should be based on a man. John Wesley was just a man. There are no "great men of God," only men who serve a great God. John the Beloved said, *"I must decrease that He might increase."* Jesus stated that, *"without me ye can do nothing."* Amos said, *"I was no prophet, neither was I a prophet's son; but I was a herdsman, and a gatherer of sycamore fruit; and the Lord took me as I followed the flock, and The Lord said unto me, Go, prophesy unto my people Israel."*

If the church has been guilty of requiring education, titles, and degrees according to *their* standards in order to be used in the ministry in their denomination, it is very sad. God anoints and equips. John Wesley was a highly educated ordained minister, yet was empty and miserable before being converted during a small prayer meeting. If you worship education, repent. It is idolatry. For it is

177

written, *"Thou shalt worship The Lord thy God, and Him only shalt thou serve."*

"For He answered and said unto them, Well hath Esaias prophesied of you hypocrites, as it is written, This people honoureth me with their lips, but their heart is far from me. Howbeit in vain do they worship me, teaching for doctrines the commandments of men. For laying aside the commandment of God ye hold the tradition of men, as the washing of pots and cups; and many other such like things ye do. And He said unto them, full well ye reject the commandment of God that ye may keep your own tradition."

Evangelism in the 21st century, how can we do it? The answer may be summed up in a question asked by God Almighty in Jeremiah, chapter 32 verse 27, *"I am The Lord, The God of all flesh, is there anything too hard for me?"*

One Final Thing...

John 3:3 Jesus answered and said unto him, Verily, verily, I say unto thee, Except a man be born again, he cannot see the kingdom of God.

Acknowledgements

First of all, without Jesus Christ there would be neither *Life Lessons--Book One*, nor *LIGHT TRAVEL*: Lessons from the Field, Life Lessons Book Two. Without Jesus, I wouldn't be breathing. That said, there are others He used in my path, those to which I was sent, and those of whom, through their wonderful support--helped me write two books.

Three Writers' Groups: Sterling Writers Group, Stratford, CT., the Foxleaf Writers Workshop, Cookeville, TN., and Cookeville Creative Writers Group have been invaluable in their listening skills, critiquing, suggestions and support.

My Publisher//Editor/Mentor but most of all dear friend, Troy D. Smith,(Ph.D) without whom neither book would be possible...okay, they would be possible, just not probable! Thank You!

About the Author

Author of ***Life Lessons- Book One, and Life Lessons-Book Two, Light Travel:*** **Lessons from the Field**, prior to her position as a freelance writer for several media groups, Pamela Walton served as a reporter for three newspapers.

An inspirational speaker, writer and evangelical minister, Pamela Walton has brought the Gospel of Christ to those incarcerated and in the harvest field. She has served as a worship leader, visitation minister, teacher and jail chaplain.

Her life experiences and writing assignments helped provide the unique lessons found within the pages of her book: ***Life Lessons Book One***. Described by Author/Publisher Troy D. Smith, (PhD) as, "A delightful collection of essays and observations, filled with laughter, tears, and above all a keen eye for observing God's spirit working in our lives."

Her many years working on the "harvest field" provided the stories in ***Life Lessons Book Two-Light Travel:*** **Lessons from the Field.** This second work of non-fiction offers readers up-lifting true stories of those to whom she was sent on the evangelism field, as well as lessons she has learned on her journey of faith.

Witnessing the miraculous has not only transformed this author's faith, but faith in the lives of those whom have been on the receiving end of such miracles.

Excerpts from Ms. Walton's book also appear in *The Foxleaf Anthology* and *Tales from the Holler.*

Ms. Walton is a lover of all of God's creatures and is an avid Spay/Neuter advocate. She adheres to the belief that it is the only viable and humane solution to the problem of pet-overpopulation.

71334864R00102

Made in the USA
Middletown, DE
22 April 2018